A Time for Choosing

A Time for Choosing

Free Enterprise in Twenty-First Century Britain

By The Free Enterprise Group

Edited by

Kwasi Kwarteng
Conservative MP for Spelthorne

Ryan Bourne
Head of Public Policy, Institute of Economic Affairs, UK

and

Jonathan Dupont
Research Fellow, Policy Exchange, UK

First published 2015 by
PALGRAVE MACMILLAN

Palgrave Macmillan in the UK is an imprint of Macmillan Publishers Limited,
registered in England, company number 785998, of Houndmills, Basingstoke,
Hampshire RG21 6XS.

Palgrave Macmillan in the US is a division of St Martin's Press LLC,
175 Fifth Avenue, New York, NY 10010.

Palgrave Macmillan is the global academic imprint of the above companies
and has companies and representatives throughout the world.

Palgrave® and Macmillan® are registered trademarks in the United States,
the United Kingdom, Europe and other countries.

ISBN: 978–1–137–48256–3 paperback

This book is printed on paper suitable for recycling and made from fully
managed and sustained forest sources. Logging, pulping and manufacturing
processes are expected to conform to the environmental regulations of the
country of origin.

A catalogue record for this book is available from the British Library.

A catalog record for this book is available from the Library of Congress.

Contents

Foreword   vii
by Mark Littlewood

Preface   ix
by Kwasi Kwarteng MP

Introduction   1

Part I   Government

1. The Architecture of Government   21

2. The Start-Up State   42

3. A New Beveridge   60

Part II   Market

4. The Innovation Economy   91

5. The Market for Energy   112

6. Crossroads   129

Notes   152

The Free Enterprise Manifesto   172

Index   175

Foreword

The Institute of Economic Affairs exists to improve public understanding of the role markets play in solving social and economic problems. Since the IEA was founded nearly sixty years ago, we have always sought to change the climate of opinion over the long term rather than the political weather in the immediate term. We have never tempered, trimmed or amended our thinking in order to confine ourselves to whatever is deemed 'politically possible' at any given point in time.

The IEA pursues its mission in a number of ways, through an extensive research programme, dozens of events, debates and lectures every year, frequent appearances in the national media, and working closely with students and teachers and across national boundaries with like-minded think tanks across the globe.

Often, ideas put forward by the Institute have been seen as incredibly radical or politically impossible at the time, but have become accepted wisdom some years (or even decades) later. In the battle of ideas, patience is often as much of a virtue as clear thinking.

Our recent work has ranged from analysing the scale of the public debt problem to considering how supply-side reform is the real answer to the cost of living crisis, from promoting market solutions to our transport infrastructure to considering what a successful UK exit from the European Union might look like.

But our long-term, strategic approach does not preclude the IEA from working with parliamentarians from right across the political spectrum. Far from it. Whether it be to those who are already broadly committed to a free-market policy approach or to those who are merely intellectually curious and open-minded, the IEA seeks to calmly and rationally put the case for a greater role for markets and a smaller role for the state.

A particularly fruitful relationship in recent years has been with the Free Enterprise Group. Established in 2010, the FEG brings together Conservative MPs who believe a strong and clear case in favour of free enterprise needs to be made and policy developed to allow the private sector of the economy to flourish, economic growth to be increased and sustained, and self-reliance encouraged.

The FEG does not demand commitment to any particular policy positions on the part of its members. The many policy papers produced by the group are the works of individual authors, rather than a collectively agreed position. This has allowed the group to act with imagination and clarity and to make a truly impressive contribution to public debate in these challenging economic times.

This book brings together the wide range of policy proposals put forward in FEG research papers in the last four years and seeks to fill in the gaps of major policy areas not yet published on by the group in order to put forward a comprehensive programme for government.

The IEA's Head of Public Policy, Ryan Bourne, has worked closely and intensively with Kwasi Kwarteng MP, the FEG's convenor, in editing and compiling this publication.

That is not to say that IEA authors and spokespeople will agree with all of the policies contained herein. Indeed, there are no doubt a number of areas where disagreement will be substantial.

But, as a programme for government over the coming years, the ideas put forward in this book would clearly rebalance the UK towards an economy in which greater power would be exercised by free men and women in the private, productive side of the economy and less power would be wielded by politicians and bureaucrats.

The IEA is proud to have helped to provoke, shape and hone many of the ideas in this timely, radical and thought-provoking publication.

– Mark Littlewood, Institute of Economic Affairs

Preface

The Free Enterprise Group (FEG) was founded in 2011 by a small group of like-minded Conservative MPs from every wing of the party. The 2010 general election saw almost 150 new Conservative MPs elected to parliament, the largest single number of new Conservative entrants to the House of Commons since 1945. This new influx of energetic Conservative MPs quickly made an impression, by forming various groups and networks to promote thinking on a number of different issues.

The FEG seeks simply to promote the benefits of the free market, and raise Britain's global standing through hard work. Britain's success has always been built on free enterprise. In the eighteenth century London established itself as the pre-eminent global financial centre by attracting talented foreigners, often Jews and Huguenots, to engage in commerce in the City of London. In the nineteenth century rapid industrialisation saw the development of Manchester, Sheffield, Birmingham and Glasgow, among other cities, to become centres of a vast manufacturing enterprise. It was on the back of these successes that Britain emerged as a major economic and political force in the world.

Many people who believe passionately in the cause of free enterprise are conscious of this history. It was only really in the twentieth century, as a consequence of two enormous global conflicts, that the role of government was significantly enlarged, almost beyond recognition. In the challenges which face Britain at the beginning of the twenty-first century, a balance will have to be reached between the encroaching powers of the state and the capacity of free enterprise to generate enough wealth for the social provision we all want.

It is the contention of this book that too often, in our recent experience, the claims of free enterprise have been ignored. The capacity of individuals, companies and other groups to generate prosperity and well-being, when left to their own devices, is too often overlooked. We should allow a competitive and free economic environment to flourish in Britain, to challenge monopolies and oligopolies, and to allow individuals to create, innovate and take risks.

The FEG has already published a number of books and policy papers. *After the Coalition: A Conservative Agenda for Britain* (2011) was a joint work by five members looking at the future for both the UK and the Conservative Party. *Britannia Unchained: Global Lessons for Growth and Prosperity* (2012) looked outwards towards nations that are forging success in a global market and considered what lessons Britain could learn from international competitors.

In this new book, which is really a condensation of many of the discussions that we have had during the course of this parliament, we argue that the spirit of enterprise is essential for success. For Britain to prosper in today's global economy, we need a new era of responsibility for both government and individuals.

This book reflects our general commitment to the principles of free enterprise. We believe that open economies are better at creating prosperity than more socialistic alternatives. As always, it should be remembered that any publications or reports published under the FEG umbrella do not necessarily reflect the views of every member of the group.

– Kwasi Kwarteng MP

Introduction

The Great Depression and the expansion of government in the Second World War led to the discrediting of free enterprise ideas, eventually turning Britain into the 'sick man of Europe'. This was only in part reversed by the counter-revolution of the 1980s and 1990s. Today, the aftermath of the financial crisis threatens a repeat of this anti-enterprise mistake. Many worry that future challenges such as inequality, globalisation, ageing and climate change can only be met by bigger government, but this isn't the case.

Never Let a Crisis Go to Waste

For a while, it seemed, capitalism had failed. Greedy financiers had crashed the economy, leaving government budgets in crisis and unemployment soaring. Intellectuals lined up to claim that the 'era of laissez-faire' was over. Others pointed to new role models in the east, and the need to update Britain's outdated corporate methods with a new industrial policy.

This was the story we told about the Great Depression. It changed the way we thought about government and the economy. Historian Eric Hobsbawm argued that the period "destroyed economic liberalism for half a century".[1] Free enterprise, it seemed, had been shown to be just as unstable as its critics had long prophesied.

The experience of wartime only reinforced this diagnosis. If planning for war worked, why not for peace? Intellectuals from the Fabian Society had for decades been arguing for the need for greater central ownership. The two world wars shook the system up enough to allow them to give it a go. In 1913, on the eve of war, total government spending had taken up 13% of GDP. In the interwar period, it was on average double this, or 26%. In the second half of the twentieth century, the average was 42%.[2]

Even after the 1980s counter-revolution from Thatcher and Reagan, much of the post-war welfare states remained largely intact. The public sector acted in much the same way as it always had done, driven by top-down planning and centralisation. Worries about the long-term viability of public services were largely ignored. In the UK, New Labour expanded spending on health, education and in-work benefits. President Bush cut taxes, financed wars and expanded the federal control of education, without offsetting spending cuts elsewhere.

What had changed, though, was belief in the power of markets and liberalism. After the fall of the Soviet Union, even parties on the left started to accept the need for competitive markets to generate the wealth welfare systems relied on. The first tentative steps were taken to introduce the principles of choice and competition into public services. It seemed that the differences between left and right were growing ever smaller – we had reached, in Francis Fukuyama's famous prediction, *The End of History*.

And then Lehmann Brothers collapsed.

"The old order is once again giving way to another", claimed *The Guardian* commentator Will Hutton.[3] Later, he would write: "this is a terrifying moment; but it is also our generation's once-in-a-lifetime chance to change British capitalism".[4] He was not alone. For many, the global failure of the international financial system had proved that casino capitalism could not regulate itself without collapse. Mainstream economists such as Ben Bernanke and Larry Summers, who had helped define much of the economic framework of the last twenty years, began to doubt their own work. Old ideas became new again: a return to 'stimulus' and budget deficits, union power, bailouts, higher minimum wages and price controls, and, later, the need for wealth taxes, a clampdown on tax avoidance and more redistribution to put the so-called "feral rich" in their place.[5] The Great Depression had led to the New Deal, cradle-to-grave welfare, and the change in the intellectual climate that eventually resulted in the nationalisation of much of Britain's industry. History may not exactly repeat itself, but surely it could rhyme?

In 2007, on the eve of the financial crisis, left-wing writer Naomi Klein complained in her book *The Shock Doctrine* that 'neoliberals' were systematically using unexpected emergencies to smuggle in their own ideas and systems. Now, after the financial crisis, it was the left's turn. As Barack Obama's former chief of staff Rahm Emanuel famously advised, "you never want a serious crisis to go to waste". The supposed neoliberal era of Reagan and Thatcher – and, some would add, Clinton and Blair – was said to be at an end. Perhaps we weren't at *The End of History* after all.

Ideology does not change quickly, but it does change. While the Great Depression shook faith in liberalism, it was not until thirty years later that we reached the Great Society and the height of social democracy. It took another twenty years for the West to realise its mistake and begin to change course.

Now, it seems, the ideological battle between liberalism and social democracy, between free enterprise and top-down planning, is once again reasserting itself. The combination of a market economy with a social democratic welfare state is coming to an end. What political consensus there was in the last twenty years has been eroded by differing analyses of the causes and consequences of the crisis. The left has lost its limited faith in markets, calling for a return to planning, corporatism, industrial policy and price controls. The free-market right, meanwhile, is beginning to focus on substantial reforms of the state and the long-term sustainability of the public finances.

But, if this is not the first time we have faced this sort of choice, what can we learn from our past? What is the true lesson from the Great Depression?

The Great Mistake

The 1945 general election saw Britain face a more fundamental choice than, arguably, it has ever faced before or since.

On the left, the 1945 Labour manifesto argued that interwar capitalism had become too predatory: "'Hard-faced men' and their political friends kept control of the Government. They controlled the banks, the mines, the big industries ... the press ... The great inter-war slumps were not acts of God or of blind forces. They were the sure and certain result of the concentration of too much economic power in the hands of too few men."[6] It warned of the "anti-planners" in alliance with the "privileged rich". What was needed was a government prepared to "put the nation above any sectional interest, any free enterprise".

Opposing Labour, and heavily influenced by Friedrich Hayek's *The Road to Serfdom* – Conservative Central Office surrendered much of its paper ration to allow more copies to be printed – Churchill argued against the state as "the arch-employer, the arch-planner, the arch-administrator and ruler". Indeed, "This is the time for freeing energies, not stifling them. Britain's greatness has been built on character and daring, not on docility to a State machine."[7]

Churchill was no ultra-libertarian. His 1945 manifesto accepted the case for Beveridge's new system of social insurance, and that nobody should be denied access to healthcare "because he cannot afford [it]". Where Churchill differed was that he believed that "Wide play must be given to the preference and enterprise of individuals ... Medicine will be left free to develop along its own lines. Liberty is an essential condition of scientific progress."

Churchill lost – both the argument and the election. A new paradigm of government intervention in the economy – the 'New Jerusalem' – was set for future governments on both the left and the right. The government would create a new over-arching welfare state, manage demand along Keynesian lines to maintain full employment, and take over many of the economy's leading industries. At one point or another, Britain has nationalised its trains, buses, lorries, canals, aeroplanes, airports, airlines, housing, land, radio, television, telephones, water, electricity, coal, gas, oil, steel, banks, hospitals, cars and even, in Thomas Cook, its travel agent.

Given the intellectual climate, it is not such a surprise that Britain made the choice that it did. Most believed the simple story that would be repeated for decades in history books. Unbridled corporate greed on Wall Street had led to a crash in world markets which had facilitated the onset of the Great Depression. Obsessed with balancing budgets, governments tried to end the recession through cuts to public spending and benefits, making the problem worse. What was needed was higher deficit spending, greater public investment and more central planning.

The experience of wartime, it was thought, had shown that co-ordination was more efficient than competition. A key contributor to the war effort had come from the economies of scale of centrally planned mass production: standardised parts, specialised factories and manufacture in bulk. The German craft style of small, artisan production was unable to keep up. Wartime rationing had had helped ensure a fair allocation of essential resources, unrelated to wealth, while the nationalisation of the railways had shown that they could run without profit.

As the leading economic textbooks argued, given its faster growth rate, it was only a matter of time before the Soviet Union overtook the US. The British government had to take a firmer hand to tackle Beveridge's five 'Giant Evils' of Want, Disease, Squalor, Ignorance and Idleness. The state would create a 'cradle-to-grave' welfare system; nationalise the health service; build 200,000 houses a year, but prevent land owners from developing their own land without 'planning permission'; make secondary education compulsory until the age of fifteen; and seek a full-employment economy.

For a time, this new model seemed to work. From 1947 to 1969, the US averaged growth of 2.2% per capita, more than double the interwar average. The emerging economies of the day, in recovering Western Europe, enjoyed catch-up growth on average of 4.4%. Even the UK enjoyed strong growth of 2% per annum. There were few fundamentally new innovations – computers, nuclear power and jet engines all resulted from the war – but the so-called 'Golden Era' saw the spread of what we now think of the basics of modern life: cars, modern household appliances and, of course, television.

By the 1970s, though, the post-war boom had run out of steam. Britain found itself overtaken by many of its rivals on the continent. The 'sick man of Europe', however, was far from alone. The 1960s saw rapidly climbing crime rates across the West, followed a decade later by slowing growth, soaring inflation and creeping unemployment. Country after country began to hit the limits of Keynesian social democracy. By the early 1980s, Sweden was entering its second 'lost decade', inflation had passed 400% in Israel, and Australia's finance minister was warning that his country was in danger of becoming a 'banana republic'.

People began to question again what had really gone wrong in the 1930s. Economists Milton Friedman and Anna Schwartz had argued that it had not been a greedy Wall Street that broke the economy, but a shrinking money supply. Later economists pointed to the role of a poorly managed gold standard in transmitting the shock across the world. As Ben Bernanke wrote in 1995, summarising the academic consensus, "To an overwhelming degree, the evidence shows that countries that left the gold standard recovered from the Depression more quickly than countries that remained on gold. Indeed, no country exhibited significant economic recovery while remaining on the gold standard."[8] Countries such as Spain (which never joined), the sterling bloc and the Scandinavian countries (which left shortly after Britain) did relatively well. Countries that followed France in remaining part of the Gold Bloc, such as the Netherlands and Italy, did relatively badly.

In other words, it was not free enterprise that brought about the crash or the persistent recession, unemployment and political instability that were to follow. It was the failure of governments in their application of monetary or exchange-rate policy. Much of the intellectual justification for Britain's turn towards the big state had been based upon a mistake.

As for the danger of balanced budgets, Labour Chancellor Philip Snowden's 'austerity' package of 1931, cutting cash spending by 9% over two years, was followed by one the most dramatic falls ever experienced in British unemployment. Despite Keynes's predictions that "the direct effect on employment must be disastrous...it is safe to predict that it will increase the volume of unemployment",[9] unemployment actually fell from 15% in 1931 to 12% by 1934.[10] Supported by cheap money and unencumbered by post-war planning laws, Britain saw a housing boom, building 2.8 million new homes across the decade.[11]

While politicians' commitment to balanced budgets may have been benign, their faith in planning had more serious implications. The 1930s saw a distinct move away from competition. Governments of the 1930s encouraged the shipbuilding, iron and steel industries to buy each other out. The Coal Mine Act of 1930 promised workers shorter hours if they agreed to cartelisation, while, later, the committee that set tariffs promised more generous protection to industries that consolidated further. By the mid-1930s, half of manufacturing output was produced under a cartel.[12] After the war, governments went further, picking winners through 'national champions', tariffs and industrial subsidies. The long-term effect of limiting competition was to slow growth.[13] By fingering the wrong culprit, politicians ironically helped bring about exactly what they were trying to avoid: a declining Britain.

Desperately trying to restore the good times, the establishment in the 1970s redoubled their efforts on Keynesian methods. They tried to jumpstart the economy through higher budget deficits and easy monetary policy. The West in general, and Britain in particular, however, were still too dominated by regulation, inefficient government industries and unco-operative unions. Without putting in the hard work of supply-side reform first, the sugar rush of stimulus just led to ever higher inflation.

The 1980s are often seen as the time when classical liberal ideas staged a counter-revolution, driven by right-wing politicians such as Thatcher and Reagan. While this is true, it is important to note that this phenomenon affected many more than just two countries. Across the world, inflation was conquered, government monopolies were privatised and tax rates were cut. This happened not just under the right in the UK and the US, but under the left in Australia and Canada, under the Nordic Social Democrats, and even, to some extent, in continental Europe.[14] The world's governments did not shift away from social democratic ideas because of some right-wing conspiracy, but because the old interventionist policies did not work.

Even more dramatically, after finally accepting the need to open up their markets, the long-dormant giants of China and India finally began to catch up with the West. In the thirty years between 1950 and 1980, Chinese GDP per capita roughly doubled, growing about 3% a year. In the thirty years after 1980, it went up by a factor of ten, growing more than twice as fast, at 8% a year.[15]

As we now know, the economic Great Moderation was brought to an end by a new financial crisis. Once again, thinkers on the left pointed to the recession as a proof of the wider failure of free enterprise. "The three-decade neoliberal experiment ended in global financial crisis", argues Labour peer and Oxford academic Stewart Wood. Now free enterprise, rather than communism, was "the god that failed".[16] It created under-regulated markets, predatory oligopolies and growing inequality. The New Labour solution of redistribution through ever higher benefits and tax credits has reached its end. Instead, Wood and his fellow thinkers believe, we need to undertake more 'predistribution', interfering with the structure of markets and forcing companies by law to pay more.

Whatever the merit of this agenda, the connection between these issues and the financial crisis seems to be a non sequitur. While there is as yet no consensus over the causes of the Great Recession, we know that whatever happened was not simply the result of simple 'deregulation', let alone free enterprise. Banks failed all over the world, not just in London or New York. Many of the most troubled banks, such as Bear Stearns or Lehman Brothers, were stand-alone investment banks. A modern version of Glass–Steagall separating utility and investment banking would have made little difference.

To be sure, there is blame enough in both private and public sectors. Banks took too many risks, lobbied for massive bailouts from the taxpayer, and, in cases such as the payment protection insurance (PPI) scandal, undertook widespread mis-selling. Governments mishandled monetary policy, often made matters worse through clumsy regulation, and encouraged lending to sub-prime borrowers. Given central government control of the money supply, the implicit promise of bailout and deposit insurance, banks are far from the paradigm of a free market. Free markets do not have companies that are 'too big to fail'.

Ironically, the clearest policy take-away from the crisis is precisely the importance of 'neoliberalism'. Despite disappointing growth figures, the UK's labour market has performed far better than most economists would have guessed beforehand. Thanks to its flexibility, unemployment has not risen anywhere near the five million predicted by some Keynesians. Looking further abroad, the troubles in the Eurozone have shown the diverging performance of those countries, such as Germany, that undertook painful labour reforms and those, such as Spain or Greece, that put them off. If there is one thing we should learn from the financial crisis, it is that 'predistribution' – fixing wages and interfering in industries – is a dangerous idea, which risks hurting the young and the unemployed most.

Misdiagnosing the causes of the Great Recession could easily have just as bad long-term effects as misdiagnosing the Great Depression. But why is it that we are so keen to blame markets when something goes wrong?

The Case for Free Enterprise

Free enterprise has always had enemies. For Plato, the ideal city would have seen rule by philosopher kings, holding property in common and untainted by the temptations of base money. Shakespeare's Shylock cared so much about regaining his loan that he demanded a pound of flesh instead. In Dickens' *Hard Times*, 'self-made' industrialist Bounderby is revealed to be a selfish liar, actually given a hand up by his parents, while the smog-erupting Coketown threatens to choke out not just the environment but human sentiment. From *The Great Gatsby* to *The Wolf of Wall Street*, we have been told of the hollowness of the American Dream, and warned of the selfishness lying behind Western society.

In the ancient world, where wealth largely came from land, slaves and plunder, perhaps it was not such a surprise that many saw all wealth as exploitation, or that the Bible warned that it is "easier for a camel to go through the eye of a needle than for someone who is rich to enter the kingdom of God". In a zero-sum world without the wonders of productivity growth, where prosperity was largely inherited and divinely ordained kings ruled, it is easy to understand why profit would be seen as greed, competition as war, uncontrolled markets as chaos.

The very idea of markets can jar with our instincts. While many species can trade favours tit-for-tat or make sacrifices for their relatives, writer Matt Ridley argues that humans are almost the only species prepared to barter different types of goods.[17] If humans can do this, it does not come easily. While psychologist Jonathan Haidt argues that our innate morality thinks instinctively in terms of harm, fairness, purity and tribal structure,[18] economist Paul H. Rubin argues that we have to learn the notion of gains from trade.[19] In the hunter-gatherer world, any benefit for one group must come at the cost of someone else. The bounty from a successful hunt should be shared out as equally as possible among the tribe, to ensure that you in turn will gain when your luck falls short. Even today, few of us would make use of market norms among our immediate family or friends. You do not pay your host at a dinner party or stop giving Christmas presents just because it would be more efficient to buy your own.

At the level of a society rather than a family, many of our instincts, however, can be misguided. Our natural instincts about physics work well in everyday situations, but break down when confronted with general relativity or quantum mechanics.

In principle, a market acts as the ultimate democracy. Each time you make a purchase, you vote for what the system should make more of. The price system as a whole is our central planner, aggregating knowledge and preferences, and allocating out resources through supply and demand. Choice and competition act as our checks and balances, ensuring that companies cannot grow too lazy, out of date or inefficient.

Given certain highly unrealistic assumptions, the maths for the above model works out. It is impossible to improve on the efficiency of a 'perfectly competitive' market. Much more interesting, however, is to look at what happens in practice.

In 1955, economist Vernon L. Smith undertook a radical step for a profession more used to the blackboard than the lab. Looking to demonstrate how markets could fail without sufficient buyers and sellers, he decided to run an experiment, using undergraduates in their place. To his surprise, he discovered that, after a few rounds of trial and error, his students rapidly reached the equilibrium price that was predicted by the theoretical models. Over the next four years, he repeated this experiment again and again, varying the initial conditions.[20] Supply and demand, it turned out, worked without perfectly rational, omniscient individuals ('homo economicus'). There was no need to have dozens of firms competing – often four buyers and four sellers were enough to reach competitive equilibrium.[21] Competition, in the phrase of economist George Stigler, is a hardy weed, not a delicate flower.

Experiments from the lab, or performed solely on Western undergraduates, often fail to replicate at a macro level. The same cannot be said for the power of markets. Jumping from the smallest possible experiment to the largest macro record of history, the US proved more efficient than the Soviet Union, South Korea than North Korea, free-port Hong Kong than statist Beijing. It was not just Britain but third world nations such as India that tried to follow Fabian social democratic ideas in the post-war years, and found themselves ultimately struggling. Today's dramatic drop in world poverty has not come about because of higher trade barriers and greater development aid, but from freer trade and low taxes. A country's level of economic freedom predicts its wealth better than its supply of minerals or the quality of its education system or infrastructure.[22]

This should not be such a surprise. Markets are just one of the types of emergent order. Away from the charged areas of politics, similar ideas are not controversial. In biology, taking not insignificant inspiration from Adam Smith, Charles Darwin argued that progress in the animal kingdom came from the invisible hand of evolution, rather than a top-down designer. In academia, we have learnt that progress is more reliable when papers are subject to peer review. Democracy may not be perfect, but Plato was wrong to think that philosopher kings would be superior to the raucous competition of political parties and ideas.

Indeed, free institutions are an important component in a free-market framework. Britain would have not seen an Industrial Revolution without inclusive, stable and meritocratic institutions. The rule of law and stable property rights gave entrepreneurs the incentive to develop new ideas. A free press helped share those ideas and ensure that the country would not suffer the extreme cultural conservatism of an Imperial China. Government was under, rather than above, the law.

Today, the internet is generating example after example of order without planning. Wikipedia, it turns out, is as accurate as the Encyclopaedia Britannia.[23] User-edited Reddit gets more traffic than the *New York Times*.[24] American crowdfunding website Kickstarter has raised more money for artists than its government's National Endowment for the Arts.[25] Auction website eBay relies on transparency and user reputation to secure a fraud rate of just 0.01% on all transactions.

The limits to central planning are now well established. The real problem for philosopher kings is that planning a society is not rocket science – it's much harder. It is far easier for a physicist at NASA to land a shuttle on the moon than for a sociologist to design an effective anti-poverty programme. We cannot run a randomised controlled test on the whole macro-economy, and society contains too many factors to disentangle even with the most sophisticated of statistical analyses.[26] We know far less than we like to think.

Coming up with new ideas is not difficult, and it is rarely done for monetary gain alone. It happens in both markets and states. But, just as evolution doesn't create the initial mutations that it filters, the power of markets comes from their ability to sort those ideas that work and those that don't. If a new idea is genuinely better than the competition, the market will reward it. If something about it doesn't quite work, the market lets it fail. Prices and competition act as society's version of peer review, a way to keep innovators honest.

True innovation is disruptive, progressive in the purest sense of the term. It breaks business models, overturns cultural norms and requires rapid iteration as companies struggle to understand their new environment. It is no surprise that large, hierarchical bureaucracies often struggle to pivot fast enough to defeat initially much weaker start-ups. In the last ten years, we have seen Borders lose out to

Amazon, Blockbuster to Netflix. Half of new businesses fail in the first five years, while even one of the top 500 firms in America can expect to last just seventeen years.[27]

In the long run, this creative destruction has not just led to a complete transformation in our lifestyles. While it is easy to get depressed by today's recession, when you look at the big picture, it is hard to be anything but awed by the modern world. In the century leading up to 1814, real incomes per Briton had gone up by only 20%, leaving them with around £1,800 in today's money. In the hundred years that were to follow, from 1814 to 1914, they were to go up 250%, leading to an average income of £4,500, and in the last century they have gone up by a further factor of five.[28] As late as 1910, one in ten children wouldn't make it to their first birthday. The figure is now fewer than one in a hundred.[29] Compared with even our very recent ancestors, we live far richer, happier, healthier and safer lives.

This great increase in prosperity did not come about because of exploitation of the workers, the third world or the environment. No doubt some individuals and companies have done all these things, but this zero-sum picture cannot mathematically explain the global increase in wealth. It did not come about because of increased regulation or government intervention. Public health initiatives did important work in improving urban sanitation, but it was the wealth of the growing Industrial Revolution that was really to improve living standards and ultimately make the expanded welfare state affordable. It did not even come about, at least initially, because of advances in science. The early pioneers in the cotton industry or the inventors of the steam engine neither depended on nor had much knowledge of the latest scientific advances.

In short succession, inventors and entrepreneurs across first Britain, then the West, and finally the world developed a succession of new advances: the spinning jenny, the steam engine, railways, industrial chemistry, the internal combustion engine, electricity, and so on and on. By 1901, Britain was arguably the world's first post-agricultural society, with fewer than 10% of its workforce working the land.[30]

Just as biological evolution is often inefficient and cruel, markets are not perfect. Externalities do exist. Market outcomes are often the outcome of luck as much as effort. Individuals do make bad choices and simple mistakes. Trying to negotiate every single transaction would be impossible. Planning struggles in novel situations, but it works well when the goal is well understood and the methods tried and tested. As economist Ronald Coase famously noted, the market itself often chooses to create bubbles of top-down control within the economy – or what we call companies.

However, even when markets do fail, it is not clear that governments can do any better. As economic historian Deidre McCloskey has argued, the record of the twentieth century is that government attempts to fix the market's mistakes often make matters worse. Externalities are often better tackled by property rights and evolved institutions than top-down planning. Zoning and planning protected rich landlords rather than helping the poor. Industrial policy props up failing industries such as agriculture and small-scale retailing, raising prices for ordinary families. Regulation and high taxes led to high unemployment in Germany and Denmark, and especially in Spain and South Africa.[31]

Markets may work, many intellectuals in the twentieth century conceded, but they remain morally abhorrent, pitting us against each other in a Gordon Gekko-like extravagance of greed. More sophisticated moral philosophers such as John Rawls and Richard Dworkin sought to tear apart the philosophical foundations of classical liberalism. Nobody was responsible for the genes or the upbringing life had allocated them, and therefore nobody could be said to truly deserve the fruits of their labour. Inequality should only be tolerated to the extent that it raises the income of the poorest. Harvard philosopher Michael Sandel has argued that market norms corrupt and drive out other virtues.

If you actually look at the empirical record, such arguments seem at best irrelevant and often just wrong. Markets are more a friend of virtue than of vice. They rely on trust, co-operation and mutual empathy. You can't have a free-market society without a rule of law – which is perhaps why England was the first society to see both an Industrial Revolution and sharply declining homicide rates.[32] The rich have always been able to afford luxuries, but it is markets that have given the poor food and shelter. Productivity growth means that, even if inequality increases, outcomes are not zero-sum.

Markets don't care about your gender, your sexuality or the colour of your skin. If the private sector relies on greed and the public sector on duty, it is strange that it is the latter that is, on average, the better paid. It is not a coincidence that, as we have grown richer, we have also grown healthier and greener. Even artists and intellectuals thrive best under 'philistine' free markets, from Plato in Athens to Michelangelo in Florence or Rembrandt in Amsterdam.

Two Paths for Britain

Britain's success has been built on free enterprise. Yet, while in many emerging economies markets are viewed as a source of liberation, in Britain they are regarded with scepticism. All too often they have taken the blame for anything that goes wrong, from bankers' bonuses to high fuel bills. The financial crisis dredged up many old critiques of capitalism, many of which were last abandoned after decades of painful experience. In order to avoid the same mistakes, we have to continually recast the argument for free enterprise for a new age.

But it is not enough simply to address arguments about the past. Even among those who accept the positive role of economic liberalism in the twentieth century, many now believe that the challenges of the twenty-first century cannot be solved by markets alone. The new critics of free enterprise believe that markets have no answers to the structural trends shaping our future: inequality, globalisation, ageing and climate change. Together, they believe, these forces will create a highly unstable and unequal economy, solvable only by an ever-growing state.

One fear comes from changing technology. Some argue that we are on the verge of a technological revolution, which will automate away many of today's jobs. One recent paper suggested that in the next couple of decades up to 47% of US jobs are at risk.[33] The supermarket self-checkout and the airport self-check-in stand as a signal of what's to come. Even if the impact is less dramatic than this, many worry that accelerating technology will increasingly benefit the already talented, further driving up inequality.

Somewhat contradictorily, an equally prevalent worry is that the West faces a stagnation, turning society into a zero-sum contest. This stagnation comes in many types. Some, such as Robert Gordon, believe that we are facing diminishing returns from technological progress. Larry Summers, by contrast, believes that our economy is structurally unable to provide enough demand, and that the government will have to take over much of our investment.

Whatever happens to technology, it is certainly true that some areas of our economy seem stagnant. Government productivity remains flat. House price inflation has been around 5,000% since 1969.[34] While only 2.3% of England's surface may theoretically be built over,[35] the restrictions of the 1947 Town and Country Planning Act have ensured that land remains in scarce supply. Globally, commodity prices have soared in the last decade, increasing three times over after being largely static in the decade before.[36]

One reason for the pressure on resources is that, at long last, developing giants such as China and India are beginning to catch up with Western standard of living and productivity. As recently as 1980, emerging economies produced about 31% of total world output, while today's G7 produced 56%. By 2018, this is expected to have basically flipped, with the G7 producing 35% and emerging economies 54%.[37] Pessimists worry that the inevitable result will be a cut in wages for low-skilled workers in developed countries as they face an onslaught of new competition.

On top of this, the ageing West faces a significant demographic disadvantage compared with the still-young developing world. Increasing life expectancy, static pension ages and falling birth rates have led to rich countries facing an ever-lower ratio between the working population and those who rely on them. In 1950, a man reaching the age of sixty-five could look forward to, on average, twelve years of retirement. By 2000, he could expect nineteen years, and by 2050 it will be twenty-six.[38] The 2013 Fiscal Sustainability Report by the Office of Budget Responsibility suggested that, over the next fifty years, even making heroically optimistic forecasts about increases in health productivity, an older population will cost an additional 5% of GDP a year.[39] Without significant reforms or higher taxes, the combination of cost pressures and demographics means that Britain's deficit is projected to start climbing again by the mid-2020s, and never again return to balance.

Finally, many worry about catastrophic climate change unless we rapidly cut our carbon emissions. Legally, the UK has already committed to an 80% cut in CO_2 emissions by 2050, and it is edging towards a further commitment to decarbonise its energy supply by 2030. But this, in short, would require a fundamental redesign of not just our energy supply but also transport, industry and construction.

It is easy, then, to sketch a pessimistic path for Britain's future. Our economy will become increasingly divided between the fortunate few, harvesting the riches of technology or land, and the unlucky masses, seeing their jobs stolen by robots or foreigners. In order to prevent social breakdown, the state will have to redistribute ever larger amounts from the dynamic side of the economy to the stagnant side. The public sector itself will become more expensive as it struggles to deal with an ageing population and low productivity. There will have to be higher taxes on a relatively smaller working-age population, with all the negative consequences this brings for incentives to work and invest. The "greatest and widest-ranging market failure the world has ever seen",[40] in climate change, will require a much bolder international effort to decarbonise sooner rather than later. Higher energy bills and slower growth will be a necessary price to pay. Just as in a war, the government will need to plan every element of the economy.

Coming in the aftermath of the financial crisis, this has created a perfect storm of anti-enterprise ideas: higher taxes on the rich to redistribute to the poor, and higher minimum wages to reduce inequality; industrial strategies and subsidies to protect strategically important industries; a greater role for international institutions to regulate monopolistic global corporations; more government spending to meet the demographic time bomb; taxes to target 'unearned wealth'; more government regulation of essential industries to ease the cost of living; the government becoming increasingly involved in every area of the economy to end our dependence on fossil fuels.

But is this really Britain's only path?

The lesson of the twentieth century was that many of the day's economic problems turned out to be more caused than solved by governments. When we look more closely at the assumptions lying behind these future fears, it is far from obvious that a bigger state is the right answer.

After all, is it really true that public services cannot be innovative or productive? Are resources such as housing or fuel really so limited, or could a freeing up of regulations encourage entrepreneurs to develop new supplies? Does the demographic time bomb necessitate an ever-increasing tax burden, or can we restore more individual responsibility within welfare provision? Do we need centralised regulation at a Whitehall, EU or global level, or can we allow more experimentation by devolving decisions back to communities and individuals? Can we create enough wealth to better adapt to a changing climate? Doesn't a more open, global economy require competitive tax rates and simple tax codes?

The critics are right to argue that Britain is facing a more dynamic, competitive and uncertain world. These are all reasons to rely more on markets. It will be market innovation and adaptation that delivers the well-paying jobs of the future, creates affordable public services, discovers the technology needed for clean energy, and provides Britain with world-leading industries.

The choice we face about the type of government we want is therefore becoming increasingly clear, if not always falling neatly into historic party political lines. We can have more government or less government; more regulation or less regulation; higher taxes or lower taxes; more top-down planning or more decentralisation to communities and individuals.

Governments can only operate within the constraints of public opinion, and market ideas are increasingly under attack. If we are to avoid following the mistakes of the past, the case for free enterprise must be remade.

In this book, we have attempted to look again from first principles at the major problems facing us today, gathering together the best of free enterprise ideas. What should a modern state look like, and how can we make it sustainable for the long term? What should we do to encourage a dynamic, innovative economy that equally leaves nobody behind? What are the first concrete policy steps we can start taking in the next few years?

We don't support free enterprise ideas because of greed or big-business lobbying. We support them because we believe they will make life better for everyone. Unlike governments, markets generally do not rush to take credit for their successes, and it is up to their supporters to do that for them. In the future, as in the past, it will almost certainly be free enterprise rather than the state that does most to cut poverty, create wealth, provide jobs and save lives.

The record of the past suggests that prosperity isn't inevitable. It will take a lot of work to get there from here. But, if we choose the right path, we have everything to look forward to.

PART I

Government

1   The Architecture of Government

The structure of government remains designed for a Victorian empire, centrally controlled by an elite in Whitehall. We should accept that there are limits to what a government can know, or the problems it can solve. Government should focus only on what it can do best. At the present, too many departments lead to bureaucratic sprawl. Technocratic attempts to predict the future or steer the business cycle have proved a failure. Instead, we should run balanced budgets, devolve power to increase experimentation and admit our uncertainty about the future.

The Growing State

The first reactions to the new report were, it is fair to say, controversial. The Prime Minister, Lord John Russell, complained that "in future the Board of Examiners will be in place of the Queen."[1] Queen Victoria herself worried "Where is the application of the principle of public competitions to stop?"[2] There were reports of open-mouthed astonishment in the private members' clubs of St James's Street, while another writer thought that "John Bull would be not so insane as to set up an Austrianised bureaucracy in Downing Street."[3] Its authors found themselves mercilessly parodied by both Dickens and Trollope.

Despite this controversy, the 1854 Northcote–Trevelyan report is now seen as the foundation of the British civil service. For British historian of government Peter Hennessy, it is the Whitehall Gettysburg address. In just twenty-three pages, it tore into the quality of the government machine: "It would be natural to expect that so important a profession would attract into its ranks the ablest and the most ambitious, of the youth of the country; that the keenest emulation would prevail among those who had entered it; and that such as were endowed with superior qualifications would rapidly rise to distinction and public eminence. Such, however, is by no means the case. Admission into the Civil Service is indeed eagerly sought after, but it is for the unambitious, and the indolent or incapable."

Instead of the indolent, the authors of the report believed they could create a new elite of wise, impartial leaders. It was surely no coincidence that one of the reporter's chief influences, Benjamin Jowett – he contributed a letter which was attached to the final paper – was to go on to become a famous translator of Plato's *Republic*. The reforms of the civil service came at the same time as the reforms of Oxford and Cambridge. They would create a new meritocratic entrance exam, as had already been done in India, under the influence of the ancient Chinese Imperial system. In China, applicants had to memorise 431,286 characters of Confucius and other Chinese classics.[4] In Britain, the syllabus would be much more Western, ideal for those who had studied the 'Greats' of classical thought under Jowett at Oxford.[5]

If the Northcote–Trevelyan report represented more an ideal than a programme – many of its policies were not implemented until 1870 – its belief in meritocracy over patronage came to define how the British state worked. Politicians would choose the policies, and a politically neutral, academic elite would carry them out. Whitehall would be dominated by those who had studied the Greats at Oxbridge – or, as the Modern Greats are now alternatively known, Philosophy, Politics and Economics.

Some things have changed. Over the course of the twentieth century, the British state would gradually morph from a focus on empire and warfare to welfare and planning.

The welfare state is not a new invention. As far back as the Romans, concerned emperors would hand out grain and money to the poor. They instituted public works projects, commissioning roads or aqueducts to provide jobs for the unemployed. What really was different about the twentieth century was the scale. Enjoying the new wealth created by the Industrial Revolution, governments massively expanded the safety net. In 1900, government spending on health, education and welfare made up 2% of GDP. By 2000, it was ten times bigger, or just over 20% of GDP.[6]

Not only was the state bigger, it was more centralised. The late nineteenth century saw the beginnings of the bureaucratic age. New technologies such as the railways and the telegram gave the government the ability to centralise power as never before. In 1815, it took four days for news of Wellesley's victory at Waterloo to be printed in London newspapers.[7] A hundred years later, the declaration of war in 1914 was known by the whole world within hours.[8]

Given the power of the new communications technologies and the belief in meritocratic bureaucracy, central control seemed more efficient. The old parish-based system of welfare was swept away. In the infamous words of Aneurin Bevan, 'If a bed-pan drops in any hospital corridor, the noise should reverberate through the corridors of Whitehall.'

Beyond efficiency, there was another reason to collect power more centrally. In the nineteenth century, British governments had largely believed that the market could look after itself. The only fiscal responsibility of government was to balance the budget and pay down its debts.

The Great Depression changed all this. Now, it was thought, the government could not afford to step back. Instead, it had to act like an engineer, using the budget balance to counter the excesses of the business cycle. If businesses were taking too many risks, the government should run a budget surplus. If they were, alternatively, being too cautious, hoarding too much cash, the chancellor would be positively irresponsible not to run a deficit.

By the middle of the twentieth century, the modern form of the state had been created. Voters would be allowed to choose politicians at elections every four years, and then a centralised, highly educated elite would put into place the right policies. They would control the economy to make sure there were jobs for everyone, and look after us when bad luck struck from cradle to grave.

While the pace of acceleration has slowed down, the scope of the state is still growing. It is not hard to come up with new ways of spending money, and there are constant demands for new programmes in areas government doesn't already control.

Less recognised is the opportunity cost of expanding the state. The more we spend on public services, the less we have to spend on essential infrastructure, benefits for the needy, tax cuts to boost growth, or allowing people to keep more of their own income. Even worse, in the long run a larger government sector likely slows growth. Quantifying this is difficult, but as a rough rule of thumb much of the literature suggests that each 1% of GDP rise in the size of the government slows the annual growth rate by around 0.1%.[9]

At the time of going to print, the Office for Budget Responsibility (OBR) forecasts that the state will take up 40.5% of GDP in 2014–2015 and fall to 35% of GDP by 2019–2020.[10] This is not such an impossible target – it is around the same size as the state in 2000, or the US, Switzerland or New Zealand today.[11]

When expressed as a few extra percentage points of GDP, the growth of the state can seem very abstract, of interest only to a few ideologues. What does it matter if the state takes up 35% or 40% or even 45% of GDP?

The problem is that spending has to be paid for. Some like to pretend that expanding state spending is costless, or that it can be paid for solely by new taxes on the rich.

However, as the 50p experiment showed, or as President Hollande is discovering in France, we are reaching the limits of what can be sustainably achieved by raising taxes at the top on income. That leaves taxes on wealth or profits. The latter are identified by economists as the most harmful for our long-term growth prospects; the former have been abandoned almost everywhere they have been tried – being either too broad and bureaucratic or too narrow and regarded as unfair.

In practice, then, greater spending will ultimately be paid for by ordinary families through higher income taxes, national insurance contributions, VAT or so-called 'sin taxes'. This is about as direct an increase in the cost of living as you can get. For every 1% increase in the size of the state, we need to find about an extra £19 billion in tax revenue. That's about the same as raising the main rate of income tax by 5p, or an extra £680 in tax per household.[12]

In some cases, greater state spending will be justified. But we also have to accept that the state will never be able to solve every problem. Given the limits to our knowledge, the imperfect process of politics and the fundamental trade-offs that exist in policy making, we should accept humility rather than "technocratic overconfidence".[13]

Instead of looking for ever more lands to conquer, we should be refocusing the state on what only it can do. This doesn't mean creating impoverished public services, or allowing our welfare system to fail the vulnerable. It is possible to have a much more efficient public sector and a more focused welfare state.

The first step, however, has to be looking at the architecture of government itself. Not every issue can be solved by creating a new top-down bureaucracy, or figured out on a blackboard in Whitehall.

What if we started again, and focused on government's comparative advantage? What can it do better than anyone else? What would be better to outsource, and what should it not be trying to do at all? Do we have to run everything from the centre, or we can devolve power and decision making closer to where it is implemented? What is the best way to control a modern economy? What special knowledge do politicians and civil servants have, and where should they defer to the wisdom of science or the market?

In short, how do we make a state suitable for the twenty-first century?

Streamlining Whitehall

One hundred years after the publication of the Northcote–Trevelyan Report, another Northcote was to prove almost as influential on impressions of the civil service.

As an undergraduate, Cyril Northcote Parkinson developed a lifelong interest in naval history, which was to lead him to write both nine academic books on the subject and seven thrillers in the Horatio Hornblower mode. He could not help noticing that the number of Admiralty officials had gone up by 78% between 1914 and 1928, while the number of ships fell by 67% and the number of sailors by 31%.[14] Despite a now rapidly shrinking empire, the Colonial Office had seen consistent expansion, increasing from 372 officials in 1932 to 1,661 in 1954.[15]

The explanation for this, he decided, was a phenomenon he mockingly entitled 'Parkinson's Law'. It was commonly known, he observed, that "work expands so as to fill the time available for its completion". In the same way, officials in the civil service would always choose to multiply subordinates, rather than rivals. Creating two rather than one new junior positions to take over some of his responsibilities meant that he wasn't inadvertently creating his own challenger. Once the two positions were in place, it was then necessary to think of something for his new staff to do.

Initially intended as a humorous one-off article in *The Economist*, the new law would change Parkinson's life. It would go on to be published as a best-selling book, to be adapted by the BBC into a musical and by the Czechoslovakian Theatre Company into a dramatisation. (Parkinson was, however, saddened to find his idol, Walt Disney, turning the film rights down.[16]) It went on to inspire successor 'laws', such as the Peter Principle, that employees are promoted until they reach their 'position of incompetence', and the Dilbert Principle, that 'leadership is nature's way of removing morons from the productive flow'. Even today, Parkinson's Law remains a favourite of self-help writers everywhere, or Silicon Valley entrepreneurs preaching agile development.

It is worth, however, returning to the law's original inspiration. The UK's total of twenty separate central government departments is high by international standards.[17] The US has fifteen federal departments, Japan thirteen, Germany fourteen, while even high-spending Sweden has eight fewer ministries than Britain.

It was not always this way. Over the course of the nineteenth century, the Cabinet gradually increased in size. William Pitt the Younger's second ministry of 1804–1806 contained just twelve members, while by Henry Campbell-Banner's ministry of 1905 there were nineteen, including separate secretaries of state for Foreign Affairs, the Colonies, War, India and the Admiralty.

The first significant attempt at reorganisation came during the First World War. In 1917, a report by liberal politician Viscount Haldane argued that there was "much overlapping and consequent obscurity and confusion in the functions of the Departments of executive Government".[18] It would be best for the Cabinet to be kept "small in number – preferably ten, or at most, twelve". His personal choice would be: Finance; Defence and External Affairs; Research and Information; Production (including Agriculture, Forestry and Fisheries); Transport and Commerce; Employment; Supplies; Education; Health; and Justice.

Haldane's report, however, was buried, published in the middle of a general election. Instead of trying the hard work of restructuring, governments kept trying to add new departments, no matter how unwieldy the structure grew. Since 1979, British governments have created 25 new departments, of which only twelve now exist. By comparison, in the US, where it is much harder to make such changes, only two new departments have been created. Both still exist.[19]

Counting the number of departments is, of course, not the same as counting the parts of the state. According to the latest Whole of Government Accounts, there are around 1,500 ministerial departments, regulators, quasi-non-governmental organisations (QUANGOs), public corporations, executive agencies, academies, foundations and devolved administrations.[20]

Many multinational corporations face an equally complicated org chart. Business theorists continue to debate whether it is better to organise by product, market or function (engineering, accounting and so on). Almost no company, however, keeps twenty directors at its top table. The average size of the 'C-Suite' in US firms has doubled in the last twenty years, but remains on average around ten.[21] Small teams ensure focus and strategic coherence. It is impossible to have a real conversation in a meeting of fifty people.

While government is complex, its essential functions are relatively limited: providing national defence, securing the rule of law, running public services, collecting and redistributing money, and co-ordinating with local and external governments. Extraneous government departments encourage empire building and endless micro-policies to justify their existence. As remits overlap, accountability is reduced and contradictory policies introduced. Busyness takes the place of focusing on what matters.

The first task of many new CEOs is to update and streamline their company's org chart. We should follow the same approach with Whitehall. By abolishing or merging nine Whitehall departments, offices and agencies, the number of separate central departments could be reduced from twenty to eleven, policy integrated more closely in a range of important areas, and billions of pounds saved each year.

Some of these decisions would be obvious. The current Department for Culture, Media and Sport, for example, contains a rag-bag of largely unrelated functions and does not require a separate free-standing bureaucracy. Having been justified in recent years in regard to its Olympics functions, its proposed abolition was countered on the grounds that it was needed to secure the Olympic legacy, perhaps proving Milton Friedman's point that there is nothing as permanent as a temporary government programme. Necessary areas of government spending, like Ofcom, could be hived off into the appropriate departments. A similar exercise could be undertaken with the larger Department for Business Innovation and Skills.

Other departments could be merged. The Department for International Development, for example, often runs a shadow foreign policy with objectives inconsistent with those of the Foreign and Commonwealth Office, and it makes little sense for the Scotland, Wales and Northern Ireland offices to be separate from the Department for

Communities and Local Government. A new Department for Devolved Affairs would be much more satisfactory.

Some others would be more controversial. But, given the cross-cutting nature of criminal justice policy and wider issues that require a joined-up approach (such as deportation of foreign criminals), does it really make sense to have a Ministry of Justice separate from the Home Office? Or to have a Department for Energy and Climate Change separate from the Department for the Environment, Food and Rural Affairs?

Indeed, if governments really wanted to be ambitious for the digital age, they might even consider merging Her Majesty's Revenue and Customs (HMRC) and the Department of Work and Pensions (DWP) into a single Taxation and Payments Agency under the Treasury. Both HMRC and DWP provide an interface with households in the UK for transfers of money between the public sector and households. DWP has twenty million customers, and HMRC deals with thirty million individual taxpayers throughout the country. There are potentially large efficiency gains to be achieved by bringing together the administrative and payment infrastructure of these two organisations, including providing the public with a single online gateway to deal with payments to and from government.

These changes would make a leaner and more efficient central government. But there are some things you cannot control from the centre, no matter how streamlined your org chart.

Give Powers Back

The anger was understandable. Farmer Graham Walker, a resident of Muchelney, had seen his village in the middle of the Somerset Levels cut off since the turn of 2014 due to flooding. By 4 February he was so fed up by the response of the Environment Agency, the central government body tasked with dealing with these issues, that he let rip in an interview in the *Independent* newspaper. He explained: "It [the Environment Agency] has been worse than useless … We've told them for years that the rivers need dredging. Of course this area is going to flood in winter, but it shouldn't be this bad."[22]

Whether the Somerset Levels flooding in 2014 was simply a reaction to the sheer volume of rain, or, rather, poor policy, is still a matter of debate. Some blame the Environment Agency for its dredging policy.

Others look to EU directives setting the shape of environmental policy more broadly.[23] At best, the response of the authorities seemed slow and lethargic. But what is clear from Mr Walker's reaction to the Environment Agency's role is the powerlessness felt when key decisions are taken far away from the individuals and communities they affect.

This idea is not new. Unfortunately, though, in the post-war period there has been a significant centralisation of governmental institutions in the UK. Over the past decades, it is easy to see that power has been transferred from the UK to the EU, from departments to the Treasury, from individual hospitals and schools to departments, and from the public and local authorities to Whitehall and government QUANGOs. In the name of eliminating 'postcode lotteries', 'co-ordinating policy' and 'harmonising' regulations, more and more power has moved from communities to the centre. Minimum wages are determined by the centralised Low Pay Commission, and many wages in the public sector by national pay bargaining. Even where money is devolved in the form of block grants, the conditions and framework for how it is spent are very much dictated by centralised institutions, complete with a list of targets and expectations.

There are many theoretical justifications for why this occurs. In the post-war period, the idea of a benevolent social welfare-maximising government coupled with the vaunted benefits of centralised planning led to more centralised power. In the 1980s, Thatcher sought to centralise government in order to shrink it. More recently, the idea of putting particular functions of government outside political interference and in the hands of the 'experts' has led to a proliferation of QUANGOs. Public choice theory, which assumes that governmental actors tend to be empire builders, points out that centralisation helps to reduce future constraints on government growth.

Whatever the theory, one can see that, the more centralised the operation of government, the further away decisions are made from the people they affect, the less the accountability for the individuals in charge and the worse the scrutiny of their actions. This is true for the Environment Agency as much as for any other organisation or QUANGO.

Central planning prevents us from setting policy to meet regional circumstances or harness local knowledge. In the Eurozone, a 'one-size-fits-all' approach to monetary policy leads to significant imbalances and distortions for member countries. In the UK, a 'national' minimum wage leads to the rate being set at 70% of median hourly private sector earnings in Wales compared with just 53% in the South East, which has a similarly distortionary impact.

Local government institutions are, on average, much more likely to be responsive to local choices and communities. Moreover, devolved power allows experimentation and innovation in order to figure out what works and what doesn't. In the US, if state governments set policies which do not work or are too expensive, individuals are free to vote with their feet. Yet Organisation for Economic Co-operation and Development (OECD) figures on fiscal decentralisation suggest that local authorities in the UK have a markedly lower degree of tax autonomy than their counterparts elsewhere.

This highlights a key problem. In the UK, even those who advocate decentralisation only tend to do so in terms of government spending. But the academic literature is clear that local decision making works best when local government is given the responsibility to set taxes too. Otherwise, perverse incentives arise whereby localities are rewarded for failure via central government attempts to 'stimulate' or improve particular localities. Giving local authorities the freedom to raise their own revenues, on the other hand, creates a healthy dynamic whereby they have an incentive to be both lean and competitive. Competition between different areas stops local governments raising taxes so high that they destroy incentives for work or entrepreneurship. On the other hand, increasing growth in your area will increase your tax revenues. At the moment, it is likely only to increase the stress on local roads and public services.

Academic evidence highlights that fiscal decentralisation has a positive effect on public sector efficiency, such that a 10 percentage point increase in local government's share of national tax revenue improves public sector efficiency by around 10%.[24] For context, in the UK local government accounts for around 30% of government spending, but raises only 5% of tax revenues – one of the biggest differences in the OECD. While 95% of overall tax revenues in the UK are applied at a national government level, the figures in Canada, Switzerland and the US are all 64% or lower.[25]

As Matthew Sinclair has noted in an Institute of Economic Affairs (IEA) monograph, there is, therefore, scope for significant decentralisation of fiscal policy in the UK.[26] Business rates, for example, could be fully determined at a local level as well as giving councils more authority for revaluations and rate setting for council tax. In the longer term, a proportion of national income tax or VAT could be replaced by a local income tax or local sales tax.

Minimum wage rates could be regionalised, with the specific intention that they don't jeopardise private sector employment in the area for which they are set.[27] There is also a strong case for abolishing national pay bargaining in the public sector, whereby rigid pay scales have been applied across the country. Sweden, for example, moved from having centralised public sector pay determination to individual contracts for all public sector employees with their relevant public sector employer, which now work much more effectively.[28] Current policies in these areas have highly distortionary effects in local labour markets, particularly in 'the regions', where they hamper private sector job creation. National pay bargaining also prevents innovation within the public sector and the ability of managers to vary pay rates in order to deal with particular circumstances. Academic evidence has shown how damaging this can be in terms of healthcare provision. Areas with high private sector wages find it difficult to attract medical staff, resulting in excessive use of agency workers.[29]

In the wake of the changes introduced after the Scottish referendum, everybody recognises that the current constitutional settlement is not stable. There needs to be a better balance of autonomy and responsibility, and, while there is unlikely to be a one-size-fit-all model for every region, the general trend towards increased decentralisation is clear.

The big danger is that the opportunity to disperse power is missed. Those in central government are often reluctant to relinquish control. If politicians and civil servants like centralising control of democracy, though, that's as nothing compared with their belief that they can control the economy.

The Engineers

On 12 March 2008, Alistair Darling stood to make his first budget speech. It was only six months since Northern Rock had suffered the first bank run on British soil in 150 years, and, as Darling recognised, we were in "uncertain times". Accordingly, the chancellor pledged a "responsible budget". While the budget deficit might increase fractionally from 2.6% to 2.9% of GDP in the next year, there was no reason to be alarmed. The Golden Rule to ensure current budget balance over the cycle would still be met, and growth would average 2.6% over the next five years.[30]

Just five months later, Darling had decided that instead we faced "arguably the worst [economic times]...in 60 years."[31] He was, of course, far from the only person to miss the scale of what was about to arrive, or to change their mind over the course of the year. The lowest of the twenty-four independent forecasts for growth recorded by the Treasury was –0.1% in 2008 and –1.3% in 2009.[32] (The actual numbers were –0.3% and –4.3%[33].) In February of that year, the Bank of England believed there was less than a 5% chance of growth falling below zero. While *The Economist*'s economics predictions in *The World in 2008* warned of the possibility of a 'black swan', the main examples it gave were a war with Iran and higher oil prices. The credit crunch was already priced in, with the columnist arguing that "investors may start looking to an economic rebound in 2009".[34] Eleven days before the collapse of Lehman Brothers, the members of the Monetary Policy Committee at their September meeting echoed their August judgement that the largest risk was for higher inflation.[35] Inflation proceeded to experience its most dramatic fall in sixteen years, dropping from 5.2% to 1.1% a year later.[36]

Attempting to answer the Queen's famous question – "Why did no one see it coming?" – many economists have claimed that the financial crisis was, literally, unpredictable. If it had been foreseeable, it would already have been priced into stock prices and bond yields, defeating itself. Expecting economists to foresee once-in-a-lifetime financial crises is as unreasonable, on this view, as expecting seismologists to warn of an earthquake months before it strikes.

If economists failed only in extreme tail events like the financial crisis, this would perhaps be a reasonable excuse. Unfortunately, however, Britain's deficit did not begin in 2008, and nor did its track record of over-optimistic forecasts. In successive budgets from 2003 on, the Treasury promised that the deficit would soon shrink thanks to growth in the wider economy. Instead, from 2001 it continued to expand, falling only in two years between 2005 and 2007.[37]

This record of failure did nothing to humble the forecasters. On the contrary, 2008 saw the resurrection of the old-time religion. Across the world, the conclusions of modern textbooks were thrown out.

Instead, it was time for a revival of classical Keynesian pump priming, running ever larger deficits to stimulate spending in the economy. While total tax revenues fell by £31 billion between 2008 and 2010, total spending was allowed to increase by £82 billion.[38] Only around £2.4 billion of this went on increased Jobseeker's Allowance.[39] The net result was that by 2009–2010 Britain was running a 10% deficit, by far its highest in the post-war era.[40]

This extra spending, the assumption was, would boost the rest of the economy. In 1930, Keynes famously remarked that it would be splendid if economists could be seen as "humble, competent people, on a level with dentists". Ever since, many economists have come to see themselves as not just scientists, but engineers. The economy was little more than a complex, but ultimately understandable, machine. In 1949, economist A. W. Philips created a literal hydraulic computer named MONIAC, using a series of pipes, tanks and valves to model the flow of spending around the economy.[41] This, in principle, is how economic models still work. This was the Keynesian dream: take into account enough variables, carefully study their relationships, and control over the economy would be yours.

Arguably, the most important relationship of all was the so-called multiplier. If you create 100 jobs building a new road, those workers will go on to spend their pay cheques in the local shops and businesses, creating yet more jobs in turn. A £10 billion stimulus package could theoretically generate many times this amount in increased GDP – but the question was, how much exactly? Equally important, if the government were to cut back its spending and fire those workers, how quickly would they be able to find jobs elsewhere? A high multiplier, say two or above, would imply that stimulus packages could not just support the economy, but, over time, likely pay for themselves. A low variable, by contrast, implied not just that they were ineffective, but that rapid cuts would prove harmless.

But how could you work out what this magic number was? As became painfully obvious in the post-war decades, there were no controlled experiments in economics. Economies were in the midst of continual change, as new technologies were introduced, styles of working changed and the economy was continually hit by outside shocks. There were simply not enough data points, no matter how creative your statistical technique to control for all this variation. Computers allowed the development of increasingly sophisticated models, with thousands of equations, but their end results still largely depended on the 'adjustments' creators fed them.

The multiplier for government spending in the US "is probably between 0.8 and 1.5", concluded economist Valerie Ramey, a specialist on the subject. However, "reasonable people can argue...that the data do not reject 0.5 or 2".[42] (It is almost certainly lower in the UK, where a far greater proportion of our economy depends on trade with other countries.) That is, even the most advanced economists cannot tell for sure from the data alone whether Keynesianism economics works well or not. Even worse than this, most of these estimates did not take into account the impact of monetary policy. This was like trying to predict the result of a football match while knowing only one of the teams playing.

In the real world, it is not so clear that the multiplier isn't roughly zero in most periods.[43] Imagine that the government did decide to double its deficit, sending huge new swathes of cash through the economy. This would almost inevitably raise inflation, and under its legal mandate the Bank of England would be forced to raise interest rates to try to choke it off again.

This is not just a theoretical possibility. One simple regression by Tim Congdon between changes in the structural deficit and domestic demand between 1981 and 2004 found that the relationship was basically zero, with an R^2 of 0.001.[44] More recently, Obama's stimulus bill produced fewer jobs than its original forecasts expected if it had never been tried. Equally, for all the warnings by the international community of the disastrous impact that the 'fiscal cliff' reduction in the US budget deficit was going to have at the end of 2012, American growth in 2013 was actually faster than the previous year.[45]

Before the financial crisis, most economists had reluctantly concluded that fiscal policy had little use in managing the economy. It was too slow, too cumbersome and liable to fall prey to political rather than economic concerns. Nobody, after all, believes that we should try to control the inflation target by fiddling with the level of public sector investment. "By 1995", says left-wing economic historian Brad Delong, "it was difficult to find an article in the *American Economic Review* or the *Journal of Political Economy* or the *Quarterly Journal of Economics* saying that...fiscal policy had any significant role to play in stabilizing aggregate demand."[46]

Even in cases of the so-called 'liquidity trap' where interest rates had hit zero, fiscal policy was a dangerous tool to choose for countries that had high levels of debt. Commenting on Japan's recession in 2000, Paul Krugman complained that "The government's answer has been to prop up demand with deficit spending; over the past few years Japan has been frantically building bridges to nowhere and roads it doesn't need. In the short run this policy works: in the first half of 1999, powered by a burst of public works spending, the Japanese economy grew fairly rapidly. But deficit spending on such a scale cannot go on much longer. Japan's government is already deeply in debt."[47] In another paper he argued: "Japan's long-term financial position is a bit worrisome, so keeping the economy afloat with year after year of massive deficits is a problem. And absent powerful multiplier effects, it *will* take massive deficits to keep the economy from slipping ever deeper into recession."[48]

How best to manage the economic cycle remains an important question. Some argue that we should not try to control it all, and focus on improving the economy's supply side. Even if you believe demand matters, however, there remain many options with fewer drawbacks than direct government control, even in a liquidity trap. The Bank of England could target the cash flow moving through the economy, or its nominal GDP, or simply aim for a higher inflation target. In the very worst scenario, as economists from Milton Friedman to Ben Bernanke have recognised, it could simply print more money.

The problem with fiscal policy is not just that it does not work very well. The bigger problem is that, combined with governments' over-optimism, over time it leads to a persistent ratcheting up of government spending and debt.

Economist Jeffrey Frankel has studied the difference between official forecasts of government borrowing and the actual balance by looking at the data for thirty-three countries. He found that the greater the uncertainty, the more governments took the opportunity for optimistic thinking. He found an upward bias of 0.2% of GDP for one-year forecasts of the budget balance, 0.8% for two-year forecasts and 1.5% for three-year forecasts. This bias is shared by both developed and developing countries. The UK and the US proved even worse, suffering, on average, a 3% upward bias over their three-year forecasts. As Frankel points out, this is largely equivalent to the entire deficit. Frankel did discover one class of offenders worse than the UK. When Eurozone members of the Growth and Stability Pact looked set to exceed the agreed debt limits, Frankel discovered that they were more likely to adjust their forecasts than their spending plans.[49]

One reason our forecasts are generally too optimistic is that we don't take into account the possibility of unknown unknowns. It is theoretically possible for a country to keep running a deficit and still see its debt shrink as a proportion of GDP. In today's low-inflation environment, that is much harder. Given that unexpected recessions, emergencies and wars do happen, running an absolute surplus gives more room for error. For example, the Treasury estimates that if the country suffers a shock increasing debt by 10% every eight years – not atypical – running a 1.4% deficit would see debt largely stand still at its current high of 80%. Run a 1% surplus and, by 2035, it will be closer to 50% of GDP.[50]

The good news is that, once you stop trying to use the deficit to manage the economy, responsible government finance becomes much easier. Just as the best diets set clear and hard rules, the most effective fiscal rules are the simple ones.

In the Victorian era of balanced budgets between 1830 and 1913, the UK budget deficit averaged close to zero. The UK ran a deficit of greater than 1% of GNP in only four years between 1816 and 1899, and, excluding interest payments, the average primary budget surplus was 4.6% of GDP.[51]

A modern version of the Victorian balanced budget is a pledge to balance the structural budget each and every year. This is the principle embodied in the 'debt brake' form of fiscal rule adopted by Switzerland. This still allows the budget to go up temporarily when a recession increases unemployment and reduces tax revenue. However, crucially, the allowable deficit is calculated from a formula. It does not come from political discretion.

Over the 1990s, Switzerland saw a steady increase in its debt levels. In response, in 2001 the Swiss government introduced a new 'debt brake' constitutional amendment, requiring a balanced structural budget. The amendment proved popular with the public, receiving support from a comfortable majority of 85% of the electorate.

The rule was fully implemented in 2006, and so far seems to have helped stem the nation's problem with deficits. The structural balance rule, in practice, ensures that spending grows no faster than tax revenues. Growth of government spending in Switzerland has slowed from 4.3% per year in 2003 to 2.6% now.[52]

One common misconception is that the UK's Golden Rule sought structural balance as well. The Golden Rule actually sought balance 'over the economic cycle'. It still allowed discretionary stimulus in any particular year. Stimulus today would be (theoretically) paid for by austerity tomorrow. Given governments' persistent over-optimism, this was never going to work.

Today, however, we have the independent OBR. The production of economic forecasts has been outsourced to independent experts. Doesn't this mean that the problem of inaccurate forecasts has been solved?

The Man Who Called It Right

In the words of *The Guardian*, Nate Silver was "the man who called it right". *Time* magazine called him one of the World's 100 Most Influential People, *Rolling Stone* one of its Game Changers, LGBT Magazine *Out* its Person of the Year. In 2008, he had correctly called the election result in every American state but Indiana. Now, in 2012, he achieved the full sweep, calling the winner of every state. Unlike the pundits, seeking to maintain artificial interest by pretending the race was closer than it was, on the morning of 6 November Silver gave President Obama a 90.9% chance of winning re-election.

Silver started his career as an economic consultant for KPMG. He soon gave up on the formal modelling in favour of merging his lifelong interests in statistics and baseball. Following on the heels of Bill James's 'sabermetric' revolution chronicled in Michael Lewis's *Moneyball*, he used his statistical knowledge to work out the real value of the sport's players. In 2007, frustrated by what he saw as the poor quality of political op-eds, he applied his techniques to a new sport: politics. The results speak for themselves.

For as long as there has been political thought, people have longed for expert politicians as impartial and empirical as a Nate Silver. Bought up on a classical education, the founders of the British civil service believed they could create their own version of Plato's philosopher kings through reform of Oxbridge and the new meritocratic entrance exam. Today, we seek to avoid the biases of politicians through increasingly outsourcing decisions to 'expert' bodies. It is the Bank of England, not the chancellor, that controls the most important instruments of Britain's economic policy in its money supply and interest. We rely on a Climate Change Committee to tell us the best environmental strategy, a Low Pay Commission to assess the damage from the minimum wage or an Airports Commission to predict future aviation demand. When the government wants to justify a new major infrastructure project, it first hires in an economic consultancy to build a model.

In many cases, this is a good idea. More data is better than less data. There are many decisions on which politicians don't have much relevant expertise, and day-to-day control is better handed off to specialists. Government, if anything, could use far more science rather than less. Whenever we can, we should be preferring real empirics to armchair philosophy. We should be making extensive use of randomised control trials and pilot studies, taking advantage of the government's ability to collect extensive, anonymised data.

In other cases, sophisticated models hurt more than they help. They create an illusion of certainty where caution would be wiser, and allow academics to hide prejudices in obscure mathematics. We cannot avoid the need for governments to take difficult decisions simply by pushing them out to the 'right people'. All too often, creating new institutions entrenches the aims of the policy and leads to mission creep. It is no surprise that the first chairman of the Low Pay Commission is now arguing for more powers to interfere in labour markets, as "we now know the policy has not caused unemployment".[53]

The methods used by Nate Silver were actually relatively simplistic, statistically speaking. Unfortunately, most political problems are nothing like as simple as baseball, or even political elections. Both scenarios have clear rules, a small number of important factors, and extensive amounts of repeated data, whether through many games or opinion polls.

In most important policy debates, by contrast, as entrepreneur Jim Manzi argues, we face a situation of 'causal density'.[54] There are too many factors and not enough samples to work out just from the data what is going on. In truth, most economists would be forced to admit that we have a relatively poor grasp of the scale of most of the important variables. We do not know the size of the multiplier, or, at any point in time, what the size of the 'output gap' to full employment is. We do not really know how sensitive unemployment is to the minimum wage, or what the feedback effects will be in the global climate from increased carbon emissions. We have no idea how many passengers will want to travel through our airports in fifty years, or whether self-driving cars will make new railways such as HS2 redundant. We do not know how technology will affect life expectancy in the future, or what the true shape of our demographics will be in half a century. Perhaps our current levels of debt will remain perfectly manageable, slowly inflated away, or perhaps a new financial or military emergency will see deficits spike again.

Most people claim scepticism about forecasting, taking the Yogi Berra position: it's tough to make predictions, especially about the future. Few were surprised by the revelations from sociologist Philip E. Tetlock that, when asked to make predictions about the future, government officials, academics and journalists did barely better than tossing a coin – and that the most famous pundits were often the least accurate. In a more recent example, on the eve of Russian forces entering Crimea, just 14% of 905 experts surveyed thought this likely.[55]

We have yet, however, to internalise the actual implications of this. Despite our recognition that the future is uncertain, we keep looking to experts, relying on ever more complicated models to try to get some certainty.

The OBR is a good example. It has proved a useful improvement in transparency, and in decreasing the ability of the chancellor to cook the books. Nevertheless, it has proved no more accurate at predicting the future of the economy than any other forecaster. It seeks to be politically neutral, but ultimately its final numbers are more a matter of judgement than of algorithm.

How should we deal with an uncertain future, then, in situations where we don't have enough data to follow a Nate Silver-like approach?

One answer is to be as cautious as possible. This is one reason why it is a good idea to run a balanced budget, and seek to pay debt down fast. Unfortunately, in many situations it is not clear what the cautious answer is. Is it more cautious to save the money on building a new North–South railway line, or to make sure that we don't end up with a ten-year capacity crunch?

It turns out that Nate Silver had a serious rival in both 2008 and 2012: InTrade. Founded in 2003 and effectively shut down by over-zealous regulation in 2012, the website allowed anyone on the internet to bet on the likelihood of an event, such as an election result. Depending on how you judge accuracy, in 2008 InTrade arguably had more accurate predictions than Silver himself.

These work by providing an array of contracts paying out on the occasion of some event, which are then traded by individuals. For example, you could have a contract which promised to pay out £10 if the Conservatives won a majority at the 2015 election. If you thought this likely, you would be prepared to pay above £5 for the contract. If you became more pessimistic about the party's chances, you would seek to rapidly sell the contract to someone more optimistic.

By giving a reward to those who get the right result, so-called prediction markets both encourage people to come forward with useful information and penalise those who are over-confident. This creates much better incentives than those for both political journalists and politicians, where headlines count more than long-term accuracy. As Hayek argued, one of the most important features of markets is their ability to aggregate true information. Unlike the slow and bureaucratic predictions of expert commissions, prediction markets update near-instantly. Within twenty-five minutes of Osama Bin Laden's death, and eight minutes before the media first announced the story, the probability on InTrade had risen from 7% to 99%.[56]

The success of InTrade wouldn't be a surprise to those who are familiar with the track record of other prediction markets. They are already used internally by companies such as Google, General Electric and IBM.[57] They have been shown to predict elections better than opinion polls; Oscar results better than columnists; and Hewlett Packard printer sales better than official forecasts.[58]

Nor is there anything new about the practice of betting on elections. America has had political betting since George Washington – and, by 1916, twice as much was exchanged on election betting as on the campaigns.[59] Despite the lack of modern polling techniques, later studies have found that these markets were actually much more accurate than twentieth century polling.[60]

Today's prediction markets, however, are still in their infancy. Right now, many of them are only lightly traded, blocked by over-zealous regulation and too easy to manipulate. But, as Silver himself accepts, if liquidity were higher, he would find it very, very hard to beat their forecasts.

While there are many applications for prediction markets, from future passenger numbers to terrorist attacks, a good first step would be to start, as Silver again suggests, with the basics: markets for future GDP and unemployment. Not only would this give us more accurate forecasts than the OBR; it would also give us immediate feedback on the impact of new policies. If a new policy was seen to be harmful, the market price for GDP would rapidly fall.

For more than a generation, the standard personal finance advice has been not to try to pick stocks yourself. While the market is often wrong, and there are always some outliers who beat it, for the everyday investor your best bet is to invest in an index fund. Today, government experts are much like that personal saver. They believe they can beat the market, but with little reason to suggest why their knowledge is superior.

In the modern economy, philosopher kings don't work. If it is to become more effective, Whitehall needs to be more aware of its limits. It doesn't need to personally administer every programme, make every decision centrally, steer the economy or predict the future more accurately than anyone else.

Recognising what it cannot do would allow it be more focused on what only it can do better than anyone else. That is the route to truly effective government.

THE FREE ENTERPRISE MANIFESTO – GOVERNMENT:

1) We should streamline the government, outsourcing administration, and halving the number of government departments.
2) We should regionalise the national minimum wage, abolish national pay bargaining and examine the case for significant fiscal decentralisation.
3) We should stop trying to control the business cycle with the budget deficit. Instead, we should adopt an automatic debt brake-balanced budget rule.
4) We should stop relying so heavily on fundamentally uncertain official forecasts. We should create new prediction markets to forecast GDP and unemployment.

2 The Start-Up State

Unless productivity improves, public services will become unaffordable for future generations. We can't solve this just by throwing more money at the problem. However, there is nothing fundamentally different about the public sector preventing it from taking advantage of technology or competition. The history of technology suggests that, while large bureaucracies can create new ideas, you need markets to take them to scale. We need to increase experimentation and the rewards experimentations bring. At the same time, we should free up our university system to accelerate the basic research innovation depends upon.

The Price of Music

In 1966 a ticket in a good seat to one of The Beatles' gigs in Chicago would have set you back just under six bucks. Indexed for inflation in the way that we normally calculate it, that is around $40 today.[1] Similarly, a ticket to see the Rolling Stones in 1965 from the stalls cost ten shillings,[2] or about £8 today.[3] By contrast, tickets to their fiftieth anniversary gig in 2012 started at £100.[4] Over the last fifty years, it seems, the price of Rolling Stones tickets has grown by around 20,000%. That's thirteen times faster than the rate of inflation in the economy as a whole.[5]

If, however, you were prepared to listen to the band at home, you would have faced a very different rate of inflation. A 45 rpm record of a Rolling Stones single in Britain would have cost you six shillings and eight pence back then, which is around £5.50 when adjusted by the RPI measure of inflation. Today, you can buy a Rolling Stones single from iTunes for 99p – or, if you already have a subscription to an online streaming service such as Spotify, for no direct cost at all.

While we often think of inflation as meaning uniformly higher prices, over the long term this hides as much as it reveals. One way to think about it is that we have a divided economy. In areas where innovation has progressed fastest and productivity has outpaced the rest of the economy, we have seen continual deflation. The US Bureau of Labor Statistics calculates that, adjusted for quality, televisions today cost only a twentieth of what they did twenty years back.[6] This may be a cliché, but even more remarkable than the cheapness of today's music is the power of the devices we listen to it on. Smartphones are not cheap – although they are getting more so – until you consider the cost of buying everything they can replace: a telephone, a computer, a Walkman, a library, a torch, a calculator, maps and so on.

The high inflation rate of the Rolling Stones ticket price, on the other hand, is an example of the 'cost disease' phenomenon first identified by economists William Baumol and William Bowen. Despite the huge productivity improvements we have seen in other sectors, such as manufacturing, it takes just as many man hours today to perform a Beethoven string quartet as it did 200 years ago. But, as wages have risen due to productivity improvements in the rest of the economy, the opportunity cost of dedicating your life to music rather than programming increases. Therefore, the wages that performers demand rise over time with general wages, leading to the performing arts growing ever more expensive. If you are happy to listen to a recording of the Rolling Stones, it has never been easier or cheaper to listen to a high-quality performance. If, on the other hand, you insist on listening to the live performance without the benefit of technology, you'd better start saving.

An expensive opera may be a shame, but it is hardly a disaster. What really does matter is if, as many argue, cost disease infects not just the performing arts, but much of the public sector too. Our public services are unlikely to see significant changes in the method of delivery over time, so the argument goes. We still largely teach pupils through a lecturer at a blackboard. If Thomas Aquinas were to walk into a modern university lecture hall, he would largely feel at home. We might have better drugs and new X-ray machines, but you can never replace the kindness of a nurse with a robot.

The inevitable result, in this view, is that we should expect the delivery of public sector services to become more expensive over time. We get less for more, or, in the technical phrase, declining efficiency. If we don't want to combine, in John Kenneth Galbraith's phrase, "private affluence and public squalor", we will need to spend an ever larger proportion of our GDP on the public sector. Many argue that we shouldn't worry about this – it's simply the sign of a civilised society.

This can be seen in official forecasts. The OBR's central projection is that the state will grow from a low of 38% of GDP in 2020–2021 to 43.3% in 2063–2064. This is partly a result of an ageing population, but also strongly influenced by the productivity factor. If productivity in the NHS doesn't improve, government spending is projected to rise to over half of the economy, or 54.8% of GDP.[7]

Unfortunately, measuring public sector productivity is far from easy. We can measure the inputs – such as the workers in the public sector – but it's much tougher to value the outputs these workers produce. In the market sector, the cost consumers are prepared to pay at least gives us a rough idea of value. In the public sector, we have no such clue. For many decades, believing the problem to be too hard, statisticians simply valued the output at the cost it took to produce.

Since 1998, however, and in particular since the Atkinson Review of 2005, the Office for National Statistics (ONS) has tried to construct a measure of public sector output, and hence public sector productivity. The results have not been encouraging, and seem to suggest that the 'cost disease' pessimists have a point. While productivity across the economy as a whole increased by around 20% between 1997 and 2010,[8] productivity in the public sector stayed perfectly flat, showing no increase.[9]

Perhaps, though, the disappointing productivity figures of the past decade do not pick up improvements in the quality of the services delivered? Maybe we have seen large improvements in the quality of teaching and healthcare?

Again, the evidence is not promising. Across the world, outcomes in education and health show little correlation to the amount of public money that is spent on them. Andreas Schleicher, founder of the Programme for International Student Assessment (PISA) tests, argues that spending per pupil explains less than a fifth of the differences in countries' performances.[10] The famous RAND health experiment in the 1970s suggested that increased health spending created no benefit to its recipients. We can try to judge healthcare systems by the longevity of their citizens – but this is overwhelmingly caused by differences in lifestyle, crime and accidents rather than their doctors.

Real spending on schooling has gone up by around 50% since the turn of the millennium.[11] The UK spends more on primary and secondary schools as a percentage of national income than 26 of the 32 OECD countries for which we have data.[12] While exam grades have mostly shown steady improvements, these same advances unfortunately disappear on other, external measures. Research by Professor Robert Coe of Durham University suggests that A levels are now two grades easier than they were twenty years ago.[13] The 2011 OECD Economy Survey of the UK complained that "The share of A-level entries awarded grade A has risen continuously for 18 years and has roughly trebled since 1980 ... independent surveys of cognitive skills do not support this development." You can never get a perfect comparison from international surveys such as PISA, but it is difficult to deny that British education has, at best, stagnated.

Having a generous, reliable health system and universal education is no doubt important. It is difficult to deny, however, that, whichever way you look at it, we are not getting the bang for our buck from the public services. Despite decades of attempt by governments to introduce ever more 'reform', cost disease seems to be winning.

But is this pessimistic outlook really inevitable? Are all public services like a live musical performance – or could they be more like a digital single?

It is not as if there are not intriguing possibilities, many of which are already being experimented with.

In education, reformers talk of 'flipping the classroom', with pupils learning and constantly monitored by digital technology, while teachers focus on helping those struggling with their homework. Rather than get feedback once every few years, parents could log in every day to see how their child is doing. Learning can be personalised. If someone is struggling to learn the normal distribution, they can be directed to a short video by a world-leading tutor or a chat room to work it through with assistance – and then be automatically tested every few weeks to see whether they still remember. If, on the other hand, someone has already mastered the basic material, there is no reason why they need to be held back by the rest of the class preventing them from going further and deeper.

In health, the cost of sequencing the human genome has fallen faster than the cost of computer power. Stem cells have already been used to replace a patient's windpipe, with scientists now working on growing heart tissue.[14] The next big wave of technology looks set to focus on wearables, individual data and the potential for your mobile to monitor your overall fitness. As the cliché goes, prevention is better than cure. Understanding our own genetic inheritance or simply monitoring our body more closely will allow us to better address problems before they become serious. 'Crowdsourcing' our medical data – sharing it in anonymised form online – will give medical researchers a much larger supply of data to work from, and help create a more accurate knowledge base. (At the moment, one pessimistic estimate suggests that most published research findings are false.[15])

Across the public sector, greater portability and transparency of data could make it easier to identify where problems are, reduce errors and tackle fraud. In crime and justice, we are already all too aware of the ability of the state to oversee our activities – if anything, many would like it to be rather less effective. It will be especially important in the coming decades to ensure that the digital revolution doesn't just make it easier for governments to monitor their citizens, but also for citizens to monitor their governments.

But, even without profound technological advances, we should not become complacent about the quality of today's public services or ignore the low-hanging fruit for improvements. Just comparing individuals or institutions against each other, or our performance against other nations, we know we have massive room to improve. We know that there are massive inequalities in life expectancy between rich and poor, that cancer survival rates in the NHS are internationally low and that our pupils are falling behind Canada and Finland, let alone Singapore or Korea. There may be genetic or environmental reasons why not everyone can be equally healthy or talented, but we should err on the side of ambition.

Why not seek a society where everyone is fluent in the basics of mathematics, history, literature and science? We should be aiming for a society of grade *deflation*, where exams are able to get harder, not easier. Many worry about increased inequality in the twenty-first century as the benefits of growth go to those able to master new technologies. One way to address this is to radically improve the education of maths, statistics and programming in our schools. Some patronisingly worry that the majority of pupils wouldn't able to handle more maths – but if such a limit exists, we are far from it. In 2009, just 1.7% of fifteen-year-olds in England achieved Level 6 on the international PISA test, compared with 5% in Finland and Germany, 8% in Singapore and 27% in Shanghai.[16]

It is easy, of course, to argue in principle for adoption of best practice in public service provision, for more competitive methods and increased use of technology. But what does it take to make it really effective? It is not as if schools have been ignoring the existence of computers or the internet. Previous projects, just like Labour's attempt to build a NHS database, have not exactly been encouraging.

What would it take to make government tech so efficient that the cost of the public sector actually comes down? How can we make the state as innovative as a Silicon Valley start-up?

The Start-Up State

If there is one location that represents the height of Silicon Valley ambition, it is Google's skunkworks labs: Google X. Rather than seek gradual improvement, it experiments with 'moonshots' – disruptive technologies that have the potential to fundamentally change our way of living. Its projects read like the prop list from a science fiction movie: augmented reality glasses, a 16,000 core virtual brain, or high-altitude hot air balloons providing internet access to rural areas.

Sebastian Thrun was both the co-founder of Google X and the lead manager on its most famous project of all, the self-driving car. German-born, the Stanford professor shot to fame after his team's car Stanley won the second Defense Advanced Research Projects Agency (DARPA) Grand Challenge, driving itself seven miles through the Mojave Desert. Hired by Google in 2007 to help with its Street View project, Thrun went on to develop first Google's own self-driving car and then the wider Google X lab.

Thrun had a scientist's dream job: his own research lab, near-complete freedom and the resources of the world's most successful internet company at his disposal. Then in 2012 he stepped down, moving to a hands-off board position. He was focused on an even bigger project than cars that could drive themselves: higher education.

The path to Thrun's job change began in early 2011, when the scientist was due to speak at an annual TED conference in Long Beach, California. Sitting in the audience, he heard the story of Salman Khan, a young hedge fund analyst whose short YouTube lessons went on to be watched over 390 million times.[17] Deciding to give it a go himself, Thrun opened up his own Stanford Artificial Intelligence course to the world. Over 160,000 people took him up. While the majority dropped out, none of the 400 top students on the final exam came from Stanford.[18] Within a year, Thrun was giving in his notice to Larry

Page and Sergey Brin, so that he could focus on his new educational start-up, Udacity.

Together with Khan, Thrun became the lodestar for what was to become awkwardly entitled the 'massive open online course', or MOOC. No more would access to the best education be rationed to the tiny minority who could fit in the lecture halls. Given access to the internet and a cheap computer, even a child in Africa would soon have access to the world's best teachers from Stanford or Oxford. A thousand-year-old institution was finally being disrupted. Seeking to catch up, Harvard and MIT joined together to create edX. Coursera, another start-up provider, was soon "growing faster than Facebook". The year 2012, in the words of a breathless *New York Times* headline, was to be "the Year of the MOOC".[19]

And yet, almost immediately after the hype came the scepticism. Distance learning was nothing new. The Open University has existed since 1969, and much of what supposedly makes MOOCs special has been possible since the invention of the gramophone, if not the printing press. Correspondence courses have existed since the nineteenth century.

Perhaps most damning of all, it turned out that even Sebastian Thrun, Google's top man, was struggling. In an extended interview with Fast Company in late 2013, he admitted: "I'd aspired to give people a profound education – to teach them something substantial. ... but the data was at odds with this idea ... We were on the front pages of newspapers and magazines, and at the same time, I was realizing, we don't educate people as others wished, or as I wished. We have a lousy product."[20]

It turned out that fewer than 10% of pupils who enrolled in Thrun's classes were finishing. Despite Thrun's continual attempts and experiments, he had been unable to raise this percentage. In true Silicon Valley style, he decided on a pivot for Udacity – rather than taking down the liberal arts, he would focus on a more modest goal. From now on, the company would instead focus on more vocational skills, partnering with other tech companies to develop courses to build the skills of their workers. While no doubt useful, this was hardly revolutionary. Sites like Lynda.com had been offering similar services for more than a decade.

While Oxbridge and the Ivy League are unlikely to be going anywhere in the immediate future, it is still too early to determine the fate of the MOOC. One study by William Bowen and his academic colleagues found that, in a large, randomised experiment, students enrolled in an online/hybrid statistics course learned just as much as those taking a traditional class but at a cost 36% to 57% lower than the traditional lecture.[21] As Thrun himself said in a later interview, "[it is] a process to find a good formula ... But like most of these things, it takes time to improve, to understand and to make things really good."[22]

What MOOCs do represent is a good example of the difficulty of innovation. Online learning has never been a technological problem, but a business one. How can we make a product that appeals to its end user, the student or the teacher? Is there a sustainable business model for MOOCs, or will they have to be developed on a non-profit basis? Will they be bundled together under the brand of a start-up or university? Grouped by subject or school? Perhaps we have this entirely the wrong way around, and, as economist Arnold Kling suggests, the true future is in the College of One Mentor, or COOM, in which the internet helps bring together private tutors and home students.[23]

The only way to answer these questions is with persistent trial and error. What makes Silicon Valley special is not that it contains smarter data scientists, but that it allows entrepreneurs and hackers to trial new ideas faster than anywhere else.

If there is one book that Silicon Valley is obsessed by, it is Clayton Christenson's 1997 classic *The Innovator's Dilemma – When New Technologies Cause Great Firms to Fail*. They are unable to pivot quickly enough, or to react to the arrival of disruptive technologies. Ultimately, they become replaced by hungrier, leaner start-ups. Amazon replaced Borders, Spotify replaced HMV.

Government is the ultimate incumbent. Given the realities of elections and special interests, cancelling any programme is much harder than starting it. It is the ultimate risk-averse bureaucracy, able to ignore inconvenient feedback from its equivalent of the shop floor. The lack of competitive structures and the nature of funding means that failing organisations are prevented from going bankrupt, there is nothing in the way of a 'bottom line' to consider, price mechanisms often do not operate, wages are often determined nationally, and there is strong political resistance – often through public sector trade unions, but also by objection to a 'postcode lottery' – to change.

The lifespan of private companies has been growing ever shorter. One study found that the average lifespan of a company listed in the S&P 500 has shrunk from sixty-seven years in the 1920s to fifteen years today.[24] By contrast, government functions are effectively immortal. No matter how inefficient, they cannot be allowed to fail.

While failure is invaluable, it is not inevitable, even in Silicon Valley. Many of the internet giants are now approaching middle age. They have become the incumbents – and, worse, they know it. Nervous, they look at the next generation of start-ups, and worry about being disrupted themselves. The PC revolution passed the computer crown from IBM to Microsoft, while the internet in turn handed it on to Google.

What is notable about the last decade is that, rather than gently fading away, the tech giants have chosen to disrupt themselves. Video rental chain Blockbuster was disrupted by Netflix, offering an unlimited library of DVDs by post – but it was Netflix that disrupted its own business through aggressive expansion into online streaming. Amazon rose to fame on 'killing' the book store – and then killed the book through its e-ink Kindle reader.

It turns out, then, that even large companies can disrupt themselves – and perhaps, therefore, so can governments. What is more, perhaps surprisingly, in Britain this has already happened.

The Government Digital Service (GDS) was founded in Britain in 2011 to help ensure that Britain's public services became 'digital by default'. Why was it that only half of driving licence applications were made online, while three-quarters of us bought car insurance digitally?[25] Not only would this be easier for citizens, but it could save significant money for taxpayers. A digital 'transaction' is twenty times cheaper than one made by phone, and 100 times cheaper than a face-to-face meeting.[26] Relying on simple, open standards would both cut costs and make it easier for governments to procure work from small companies rather than getting locked into contracts with one of the large suppliers. Why was it that in 2010 the Department for Business, Innovation and Skills alone was spending more on IT than Google?[27]

GDS deliberately preached revolution rather than evolution. Its principles were those of Silicon Valley: use open standards, fail fast and learn, keep teams small but skilled. Journalists cannot help but note that its offices, with its inflatable guitar and soft toy mascot, look more like those of a Tech City start-up than an arm of the British state.[28] It is based near Holborn, not Whitehall. Its first major project (gov. uk – replacing 2,000 websites with a single unified site) started with a team of just twelve people. It went on to win a Design of the Year award and to be studied by other governments worldwide.

Its success has begun to be noticed across the Atlantic. Tim O'Reilly, a Silicon Valley Guru, went so as far as to describe GDS' principles as "the new bible for anyone working in open government…Everyone around the world should be applying this…It is as for the first time government is doing the thing that is so revolutionary in Silicon Valley – building lightweight applications so that if people don't like them…they fail.…That revolution is why we have seen rapid change [in technology]…The customer is not the government, the customer is the citizen."[29]

Across the rest of the public sector, we are starting to see the same principles applied. Over the last couple of decades, politicians from both parties have recognised that the best way to guarantee the quality of public services is to give the public a choice, and rely on competition rather than regulation to drive up quality.

In the NHS, Kenneth Clarke in the 1980s introduced the split between the purchasing and provision of healthcare, the internal market, and general practitioner (GP) 'fundholders' purchasing on behalf of their patients. After initially moving to abolish the internal market, New Labour recognised its mistake, and under Alan Milburn introduced self-governing 'foundation hospitals' and 'Payment by Results' rather than annual block payments. In 2008, patients were given the right to choose where their treatment took place, as long as the provider stuck to the official NHS price. The Coalition's 2012 Health and Social Care Act extended these forms further, once again devolving funding to GPs in "clinical commission groups", and allowing patients to choose from "any qualified provider" from either the public or the private sector. However, in other areas progress has stalled, with many hospitals still not converted to foundation status and still using the old block payment system.

In education, 1988 brought the creation of grant maintained (GM) schools, with greater freedom for their head teachers, control of their admissions and receiving a budget directly from the central government rather than the Local Education Authority (LEA). Labour converted the GM schools into 'foundation schools', once again under the control of the LEA, but also introduced the very similar 'academy' programme. While Labour restricted academies to takeovers of the worst-performing schools, the Coalition has massively expanded it across the sector. Over half of England's state secondary schools are now academies.[30] In addition, the government has introduced 'free schools', allowing parents, teachers or educational charities to create new schools with the same freedoms as an academy.

The principles behind these reforms were brought together in the 2011 Open Public Services White Paper. Across the public sector, it argues, citizens should be given choice wherever possible, money should follow the user, democratic oversight should be decentralised to the lowest level, and provision should be open to the widest range of providers.

The next stage in this agenda should be to introduce new legal rights for choice in public services and to introduce a purchaser–provider split in every area of the public sector where this is practical. We should get rid of the current artificially imposed restrictions on choice, such as fixed GP catchment areas or lists of 'preferred providers'.[31]

Many worry that introducing competition and choice into the public services will undermine the 'public sector ethos'. In Julian Le Grande's terms, we often talk of public servants as altruistic 'knights' in contrast to selfish 'knaves', dedicated to the welfare of the 'pawns' below them.

But the real world is more complicated than this. There are selfish and selfless doctors, just as there are selfish and selfless entrepreneurs, artists or, for that matter, bankers. It is deeply patronising to argue that adults are incapable of choosing their healthcare or the education of their children. There is no real trade-off between choice and compassion. When you give teachers a pay rise, they do not start caring about their pupils any less. The failure of any institution, whether it be a school, a business or a hospital, is sad. What is far worse, however, is to let failing institutions continue for generations.

The easiest win in improving our education system would be simply to raise the level of the bottom performers. As in the private sector, often that may mean letting some institutions fail and be replaced. At the moment, around a quarter of primary schools see over a quarter of their pupils unprepared for secondary school, while other schools see fewer than 5% of pupils do so badly.[32] Good schools exist in both deprived and wealthy areas. It is teaching and management quality that is the real bottleneck. Economist Eric Hanushek argues that replacing the bottom 5–8% of teachers in America with teachers of just average quality would leapfrog its current middling performance to the top of the world PISA rankings in maths and science, and create $100 trillion in value.[33]

Given the limited nature of public sector reforms so far, we have only limited direct evidence of their effectiveness. But we know there is fundamentally nothing different about health and education dooming them to rising costs. Even in America, health procedures uncontaminated by government subsidies and mandates, such as plastic surgery, have gone down in price. Lasik eye correction saw its price fall by 30% in real terms in its first decade.[34]

What evidence we do have, however, is encouraging for the reformers. Pupils in free schools in Sweden score far better than the national average in maths, science and Swedish.[35] The creation of the NHS internal market between 1991 and 1997 saw productivity increase – unsurprisingly, when it was abolished by Labour in 2002, productivity fell back again.[36] Devolution has already provided one interesting, if tragic, experiment in public policy. The new Welsh administration chose to abolish targets for hospitals and national testing for schools in favour of greater co-operation. After starting at roughly the same place as England, its hospitals fell behind in productivity and saving lives, while its pupils slid down the world league tables in maths.

Choice and competition work. But, while consumer choice and the ability to launch new ventures and see them fail are necessary for a successful start-up, they are often not sufficient.

In 2006, entrepreneur Paul Graham published an online essay, "How to Be Silicon Valley."[37] As the founder of Y Combinator, the world's most successful start-up incubator, he could claim to be one of the most qualified people alive to answer that question. So far, Y Combinator has helped launch over 500 start-ups, which have a combined value of around $14 billion.[38] His formula was simple enough: rich people and nerds.

By 'rich people', Paul Graham meant venture capital. If experimentation is Silicon Valley's first obsession, the second is scale. Once a good business model has been found, nowhere is better at rapidly injecting capital and catalysing a new firm to world domination. This, Graham argues, has to be done by private individuals, preferably with previous experience of founding companies. By contrast, trying to imitate this process through government would be a disaster: "Bureaucrats by their nature are the exact opposite sort of people from start-up investors. The idea of them making startup investments is … like mathematicians running Vogue."[39]

Unfortunately, in the public sector, the mathematicians are still firmly in control. Capital is the missing third element needed to drive innovation. Bringing in private capital would make it far easier to scale up successful academies and create new chains, sharing best practice and achieving economies of scale. Markets depend on newcomers to trial new ideas – but they also achieve their efficiency through their ability to rapidly replicate a winning formula when it is discovered. Starbucks would not have changed the world's coffee-drinking habits if it had remained a single café in Seattle.

Some critics complain that profits are inherently wasteful, and that all spending should go directly on schooling. If we took this static thinking literally, schools would never buy textbooks from private publishers or pay teachers more than the minimum wage. It is strange that at the moment we allow people to make very good money from running a chain of restaurants or hotels, but not from running a chain of schools. The lesson from the rest of the economy is that whatever we lose in a small profit margin, we gain back by orders of magnitude in terms of the efficiencies private innovation brings. The free schools programme is a welcome first step, but we need to allow the profit motive to ensure real lift-off.

Indeed, we could go further across the public sector, and encourage public agencies and corporations to earn a profit by selling their services abroad. Just as the BBC presently earns revenue through its commercial arm BBC Worldwide and private universities have started to franchise themselves, we should do more to encourage the best hospitals, schools and even QUANGOs to sell their expertise to foreign governments. Not only would this raise money, but it would subject the state to the ultimate market discipline: selling yourself to a paying customer.

So much for Paul Graham's rich people. What about the nerds?

There was another reason why Sebastian Thrun, Larry Page, Sergey Brin, William Hewitt, David Packard, Peter Thiel, Reid Hoffman, Elon Musk and Reed Hastings all ended up where they did: Stanford University.

Freeing the Universities

The US is the dominant world economy. In most of the world, we rely on American technology, eat American fast food, listen to American music and watch American films. And yet, arguably, the sector in which America is furthest ahead of the competition is higher education.

Depending on what you are looking for in a university, there are many different ways to rank the world's institutions. They all show American dominance. To take one example: in the Chinese 2013 Academic Ranking of World Universities, the US takes 8 of the top 10 spots, 17 of the top 20 and 52 of the top 100. Despite its high fees, international students overwhelmingly choose the US as their preferred study location.

What is the secret of its success?

No doubt it helps to be the richest economy in the world and speaking the lingua franca of our time. Many of the Ivy League universities have had a long time to build up an advantage in reputation and prestige, with Harvard a century and a half older than America itself. And yet this in itself is not enough to explain the advantage. Many European universities date back hundreds of years even before this, while other American universities are much more recent. Stanford, number two on the Chinese list, dates back to 1885, while number three, Berkeley, was founded in 1868. The modern University of Chicago (number nine) was founded in 1890 after a $50 million endowment from oil baron John D. Rockefeller. Reportedly, Rockefeller asked the then president of Harvard, Charles W Eliot, what he would need to create a new Harvard. He was told $50 million and 200 years. It turned out that the $50 million was enough, with Chicago one of the world's leading universities within a few decades.[40]

What really made a difference was autonomy. Unlike the state-controlled European universities, American universities had their independence. They could choose their own curriculum, how they paid their staff and which students they wanted to take. They owned their own buildings and often enjoyed their own significant endowment, ensuring that they did not rely on governments to approve their budgets. They were largely under the control of boards of trustees dominated by alumni who could be relied to focus upon the long-term interests of the university.[41]

Of course, there is another country that enjoys a disproportionate share of the world's most prestigious universities and an unusually high level of autonomy: Britain.

Universities are likely to become increasingly important to our economy in the twenty-first century for at least four reasons. First, as automation takes over a greater and greater proportion of our economy, we will need an increasingly skilled workforce. Second, the research agenda of universities is crucial to pushing forward basic science. Third, there is likely to be a huge increase in demand for UK higher education places from the growth of emerging-market middle classes. Finally, universities can provide the anchor to support a surrounding network of companies and innovation.

Although London's Tech City is competing hard for the title, the area around Cambridge is arguably Britain's Silicon Valley. As Europe's most successful tech cluster, it is already home to 1,400 high-tech companies that employ 53,000 people and earn more than £13 billion. Notable tech companies from Cambridge include ARM, Britain's equivalent to Intel, and the designers of the CPU chip at the heart of nearly every modern gadget. Beyond electronics, it has significant potential to develop world-leading technologies in agriculture, renewable energy, clean fuels and biomedicine. Along the A11 corridor are Cambridge University, the John Innes Centre, the Institute of Food Research, the UEA Climate Research unit, and a cluster of precision engineering and renewable energy expertise.

However, in order to maintain and thrive in future, the universities sector will need to address four major challenges: excessive bureaucracy; infringement upon autonomy; unnecessary government influence over research; and insecure long-term funding.

The cost to the universities sector of complying with the various quality control procedures – the Quality Assurance Agency (QAA), Codes of Conduct, and so forth – is estimated to be at least £250 million per year.[42] This would be enough to fund the academic costs of 25,000 PhD students for a year.[43] Meanwhile, unnecessary infringement upon the access policies of universities risks compromising standards, ultimately winning a Pyrrhic victory – widening access to universities but compromising the quality and value of outcomes. University admissions tutors will always have a better grasp of potential among prospective students than a government QUANGO.

The current Research Excellence Framework (REF) system for allocating research funding is an attempt to give more responsibility to academics, by submitting the judgement of "excellent research" to peer review, but the experience of academics interviewed during the course of research for this book suggested that there are frequently two unintended consequences. First, academics face unhappy incentives to produce a high quantity of research, which can then take priority over providing excellent teaching or supervision for students, which does not attract funding so easily. Second, REF encourages research in particularly 'fashionable' research areas, or can take a dim view of research that is not aligned with the dominant consensus of top academics at a particular point in time, sometimes hampering the promotion of innovation and excellence.

While the increased need for private funding for teaching has been accepted across the political spectrum, fees at their current level do not cover the full economic cost of undergraduate education at elite UK universities. Substantial funding is needed to secure the future of the universities sector, and to protect its most important aspects: wide-ranging research that competes favourably in a global context, and high-quality teaching.

As it stands, the contribution by the Higher Education Funding Council for England (HEFCE) per student to undergraduate tuition is no longer a significant proportion of the cost of teaching undergraduates. Given that fees at most UK universities are set at the cap of £9,000, individual students and their families are providing the most substantial proportion of the cost of undergraduate education. For some courses, and courses at elite institutions, even the fee combined with HEFCE grant per student does not cover the full economic cost of that individual's education.

It's becoming increasingly clear that what is needed is the development of endowments, which would create a funding source in perpetuity through income generated on investment, or drawdown of capital growth in the endowment sum. Universities could manage a wide range of assets to suit these needs, including traditional investment vehicles such as equities, but, additionally, bonds or property. The income or drawdown from endowments is, at elite institutions, already covering the gap left after the tuition fee and HEFCE grant; boosted endowments could also allow universities to cover the HEFCE grant, such that the full economic cost of undergraduate education is covered by fees plus university endowment. In order fully to replace the HEFCE tuition grants, the universities sector would need to increase total endowments by around £12 billion.[44] While Oxford and Cambridge have the largest endowments in the UK by far, a number of other universities have also developed significant sums – endowments are certainly not the preserve of only a handful of elite institutions.

This change would address a number of the problems faced by universities. First, it addresses the long-term funding problem. Giving universities financial independence reduces the economic burden on government and therefore on taxpayers, and, if this can be done in a way that does not harm universities or undergraduate education, it is clearly the preferable funding option. Second, it addresses the problem of excessive bureaucracy. Deciding student number controls and then financing undergraduate tuition through HEFCE grants comes with an additional bureaucratic price tag. Reducing the number of layers in financing undergraduate tuition will reduce these additional costs. Third, it addresses the autonomy problem. Financial and institutional independence are closely linked. Universities are sacrificing their autonomy – with respect, for example, to access as well as to fee and bursary structures – in order to continue to draw a grant, which is still insufficient in many cases.

In order to address the problem of long-term funding while maintaining international standards of quality, universities should be given greater freedom to innovate in the areas of fee structures and student support. The University of Buckingham, for example, offers two-year degrees at higher tuition fees per year, but at a lower cost overall given the lack of living costs for the third year. Alternatively, some students may wish to study for their degree over a longer period, alongside paid work or 'sandwiched' with relevant work experience. However, as it stands, the government places a standard per-year fee cap on courses. Universities therefore face perverse incentives to provide longer rather than shorter courses, regardless of teaching content.

If fee differentials were permitted, then the higher cost of subjects such as laboratory-based science and clinical medicine or dentistry – which often give the highest future earnings potential – could be reflected through comparatively higher fees, while lower-cost subjects such as arts and humanities could see fees reduced.

The same can be said for student support. Universities should be free to provide innovative support mechanisms – rather than being expected to provide certain amounts of money in bursaries, why could universities not invest in property as part of an endowment, and rent it out to students at below-market price? Such useful support would not be classed as a 'bursary' but would be a mechanism by which universities could offer practical 'in-kind' financial support to students.

We must also give universities more freedom to determine and follow their own research agendas. Government provision of research funding could be massively simplified. The current separation of the research councils, in addition to the research component of HEFCE grants, has led to high administration and running costs for these bodies, and it is realistic to expect that savings could be made in the administration costs through simplification of grant structures.

The government could still maintain projects to target funding of national importance (such as, for example, the life sciences strategy, alternative energy programmes and the global uncertainties programme). However, it is difficult to believe that existing research councils' initiatives are all of strategic national importance in this way. The justification for allocating such a large amount of funding centrally according to fixed, predetermined interests and inflexible research streams – with the associated cost of bureaucracy – is lacking.

Giving universities enhanced financial and institutional independence, through the development of endowment funds, a significant reduction of undergraduate tuition funding, freedom over access, fee structures and student support, and the reshaping of higher education governance bodies, can complete the reform of UK universities and address the key challenges faced by the higher education sector.

THE FREE ENTERPRISE MANIFESTO – PUBLIC SERVICES:

1) We should introduce new legal rights for individual choice in public services and a purchaser–provider split in every area of the public sector where this is practical.

2) We should allow free schools to generate a profit to encourage the development of new academy chains. Public bodies should be encouraged to earn extra revenue by selling their services abroad.

3) We should set universities free by giving them more autonomy over their funding, access, bursaries and research agenda.

3 A New Beveridge

The aims of the original Beveridge Report are often misinterpreted. We need to return to the principle that the welfare state is a safety net. No welfare system can create a perfectly equal society or solve every social problem. The best way to reduce inequality is by removing the regulations that often create it, from restrictions that prevent the young from being hired to planning laws that drive up house prices. We should reform our tax and welfare system to remove perverse incentives that penalise work, parenthood and saving. An ageing population will require us all to save more for our own pension and social care.

Beveridge's Revenge

> The citizens as insured persons should realise that they cannot get more than certain benefits for certain contributions ... should not be taught to regard the State as the dispenser of gifts for which no one needs to pay.
> *The Beveridge Report, 1942*

The reaction was rapturous from the start. Published a few weeks after Britain's victory at El Alamein, the Beveridge Report seemed to present a better project. Newspapers from across the political spectrum lined up to offer their support. *The Guardian* thought it "a big and fine thing", *The Times* that "Sir Williams and his colleagues have put the nation deeply in their debt." Famously, over 600,000 copies were sold worldwide.[1]

On 20 November 1942, the publication of the report on "Social insurance and allied services" heralded a radical change in our provision of welfare and public services. It has come to be seen as the start of the modern welfare state, with the belief we could, in Beveridge's words, slay the five giants of Want, Disease, Ignorance, Squalor and Idleness.

Beveridge's report was far from year zero for welfare. Alms to the poor have existed in Britain since at least medieval times, while the modern system's real genesis came with Lloyd George and his 1908

Pensions Act. Nevertheless, the Beveridge Report came to be seen as a real break with the past. In the words of *The Times*, it provided "a confident assurance that the poor need not always be with us". What really excited people was the report's vision that in the near future the hated means testing of benefits could disappear.

For a while, the initial enthusiasm surrounding the Beveridge-inspired welfare state seemed warranted. In 1950–1951, the acclaimed poverty researcher Benjamin Seebohm Rowntree published a sequel to his famous studies of working-class poverty in York, which had revealed shockingly high levels of abject poverty amidst relative affluence. The 1950 study produced radically different results: poverty, at least under Rowntree's austere definition of the term, was on the brink of being eradicated. This was widely heralded as the 'ending of poverty', and to a large extent attributed to the new welfare settlement.[2]

Seventy years on, the challenges we face are very different from war-torn Britain: yet, in many ways, we face the same crisis of how to provide for an entirely new landscape in the twenty-first century. There's widespread recognition across the political spectrum of the need for a new welfare settlement. Yet, while substantial support is expressed across the political spectrum for a return to Beveridge's original principles, many politicians still labour under a misapprehension as to what these principles are.[3]

Beveridge's report has been hijacked ever since its publication. Beveridge was not the socialist Robin Hood figure of modern left-wing legend. Rather, he was an austere economist, versed in the principles of contribution and industry. He wanted to build a system of social insurance that would reward the industrious, not punish them in favour of the indolent. Many of Beveridge's statements would be considered controversial today, especially among those who habitually invoke his name.

Attempts to, for example, raise employment levels among welfare recipients by expecting participation in work-focused activities are viewed with great suspicion by such contemporary groups: they are seen as thinly disguised attempts to blame poverty on the poor themselves, and foster negative attitudes towards them.[4] This is a mindset which Beveridge would have found bewildering. He did not see the poor as being helpless victims of circumstances beyond their control, to whom the state owes unconditional support, and of whom the state must demand nothing lest it might overexert them.

Reportedly, he even hated the phrase 'welfare state', believing it suggested a 'Santa Claus' state.

Beveridge's original aims and ambitions were very different from what the welfare state ended up being.

The introduction to the Beveridge Report explained the way that the new system should operate, in abstract terms:

> social security must be achieved by co-operation between the State and the individual. The State should offer security for service and contribution. The State in organising security should not stifle incentive, opportunity, responsibility; in establishing a national minimum, it should leave room and encouragement for voluntary action by each individual to provide more than that minimum for himself and his family.

It also made a clear appeal to duty and obligation on the part of the beneficiaries:

> The higher the benefits provided out of a common fund for unmerited misfortune, the higher must be the citizen's obligation not to draw upon that fund unnecessarily.

Underlying the principle of benefit comes a duty on the part of the individual to bear responsibility for their own life and well-being – with the state serving as a guarantor of this freedom rather than a supplier of it.

Crucially, Beveridge also wanted to ensure that there was a carrot and a stick:

> The correlative of the State's undertaking to ensure adequate benefit for unavoidable interruption of earnings, however long, is enforcement of the citizen's obligation to seek and accept all reasonable opportunities of work, to co-operate in measures designed to save him from habituation to idleness, and to take all proper measures to be well.

For the contributory principle to function, Beveridge also believed that this ruled out means testing, feeling that people would object to being punished for saving independently if it then meant they were ineligible for benefits. His axiom was that

> Payment of a substantial part of the cost of benefit as a contribution irrespective of the means of the contributor is the firm basis of a claim to benefit irrespective of means.

Indeed, this is the basis of the two options that Beveridge sets out for funding – taxation and insurance contribution – and, as he explains, the reason for his choosing the latter.

> The distinction between taxation and insurance contribution of that taxation is or should be related to assumed capacity to pay rather than to the value of what the payer may be expected to receive, while insurance contributions are or should be related to the value of the benefits and not to capacity to pay.

In truth, some of the seeds of the failure of Beveridge's vision were sown in his own recommendations, or at least soon after its implementation. Beveridge envisaged a single flat-rate payment paid by all for a single flat-rate level of benefit in unemployment set to meet living costs. As such, the aim of the system was for the state to set a minimum safety net, with individuals able to undertake further provision, if they so desired. The new pensions system was to be introduced over a twenty-year period, and on a fully funded basis.

As we now know, the contributory principle – a central tenet of Beveridge's original report – has long since been discarded. Successive British governments have been complicit in eroding the link between contributions and payments, while simultaneously convincing individual taxpayers that it still exists. Many people still believe, even now, that if you pay your national insurance contributions you have built up an entitlement to benefits, healthcare and so forth. This is only a partial truth.

Only a small share of working-age benefit payments bear any relationship to the recipient's prior contribution record, and even among those, the link is often a weak one. Some benefits, for example 'contribution-based' Jobseekers' Allowance (as opposed to the income-based version of JSA), are contributory in name only.[5]

National insurance contributions and taxes paid by working people today are used to pay for pensions for the retired. This pay-as-you-go system is unsustainable in its current form when you consider the projected changes in our population, with the proportion of working-age people shrinking considerably. Beveridge's hope that means testing would eventually fade away seems as distant as ever, while his crucial assumption that the economy would largely enjoy full employment proved over-optimistic.

Over time, the welfare system has moved away from work-based insurance and has instead become a vehicle for redistribution to various groups. Of course, a work-based welfare scheme naturally struggles to deal with those with disabilities, for whom extra assistance will always be required. There will also always be a debate over whether the welfare state influenced types of family formation or whether the more generous benefits to lone parents, for example, were simply a reaction to societal trends.

A more recent trend has been the extensive churn introduced into the system. The propensity to use the tax and benefits system to take money from people, then return it to them based on various formulas, as in the case of tax credits, has massively increased.

On 2 December 2013, 4.6 million families were either tax credit recipients or receiving the equivalent child support through benefits.[6] A client state fuels demand for further state clientelism. Tax credits, for example, were originally introduced to encourage work, but this emphasis soon faded. The former Working Families' Tax Credit was split into the Working Tax Credit and the Child Tax Credit, and the latter – by far the most significant component – comes with no work requirement at all. In many cases, tax credits either subsidise shorter working hours or the amount an employer is willing to pay. This leads to further demands for more stringent regulations on work, such as higher minimum wages.

All this has meant that the size of the welfare state has grown hugely. Since its implementation in 1948, the amount spent on welfare has increased more than 17 times in real terms, from £12 billion to £208 billion.[7] Strains on the welfare state are often blamed on benefits being too generous, but the truth is that welfare is so expensive – over £90 billion for working-age benefits alone – because too many people are eligible. In fact, JSA – the main out-of-work benefit – is fairly stingy for those who have contributed to the tax system for years and find themselves out of work for the first time. Yet 68% of all children now live in a household which receives at least one major type of income transfer, not even counting the quasi-universal Child Benefit. Welfare spending has long ceased to be limited to the poor, however defined. On average, households in the middle quintile of the income distribution receive a quarter of their income in the form of state transfers.[8] Widespread eligibility explains a greater share of the large increase in spending than 'excessive' generosity.

Of course, not all of these changes can be laid at the door of a badly designed system. Beveridge lived in a time when, in the words of the Institute for Fiscal Studies, "men worked and married women didn't, the only single parents were widows, and life expectancy was lower than the pension age." When Beveridge wrote his report, fewer than 5% of births were outside marriage. The figure is now one in five.[9]

Despite all this, however, the underlying principles of the Beveridge system have strong appeal today. While we should provide a safety net that nobody can slip through, the best way out of poverty is work. Lest it be abused, welfare should not be seen as a right or a gift, but something that is earned. If it is to prove sustainable over the long term, it must be kept affordable.

In the coming decades, the welfare state will face new challenges. An ever-ageing population will put increasing pressure on the budgets of welfare and public services. New technology and a globalised world will disrupt many of today's jobs, forcing workers to become more flexible and change career more often.

How can we adapt to these changes, while still retaining the essential values of welfare? Can we fix the flaws in the original report, and adapt the system to make sure the combined effect of our tax and welfare systems is suited to the modern needs of families?

The Temporary Tax

It was, William Pitt explained, necessary for the "national honour and the national safety".[10] While the prime minister still believed that taxation should ideally be on expenditure, such taxes were too open to avoidance. He had tried increasing the taxes on auctions, bricks, nuts, spirits, sugar, teas, coffee, clocks, stage coaches, newspapers, almanacs, bonds, passports, wills, wigs, advertisements, fire insurance, horses and female servants.[11] All these had proved not to be enough. Given the burgeoning costs of the war against Napoleon, the only solution was a new source of revenue: income tax.

From the beginning, it was controversial. It went against the advice of the leading economist of the day, Adam Smith, to avoid direct taxes on income, and that taxes on luxuries should be optional. It required uncomfortable breaches of privacy. As one doctor asked, 'Are the fruits of a man's labour to be picked over, farthing by farthing, by the pimply minions of Bureaucracy?'[12] Nearly 400 petitions were received by Westminster, calling on them to abandon it.[13]

In response, Pitt announced that the tax was only to be temporary, an emergency measure for wartime. The temporary peace of Amiens saw it cancelled, only for the renewal of war in 1803 to see it resurrected again. Victory at Waterloo saw it once again abolished in 1816, with "a thundering peal of audience" and related documents destroyed.

Strangely, however, the 'temporary' tax showed remarkable staying power. In 1842, Robert Peel reintroduced the income tax, again for a temporary three-year period while the deficit was being paid down. The deadline came and went. In 1853, Gladstone committed to abolishing the income tax by 1860. In 1858, Disraeli argued that the "unjust, unequal and inquisitorial" tax should only "continue for a limited time". It is still there today – and theoretically still temporary, abolished every year on 5 April.

This was probably inevitable. Income tax proved too efficient a means of collecting revenue for governments to ignore. America, Japan, Australia and other European countries followed Britain's lead in the second half of the nineteenth century.

Over the course of the twentieth century, income tax paid for the welfare state. The size of the British state increased from around 15% of GDP in 1900 to 40% at the century's end.[14] Income tax was the principal means of financing this expansion. In 1914, the standard rate was 6%. By 1918, it had reached 30%. In 1938, only four million taxpayers paid income tax.[15] By the end of the century, twenty-seven million individuals were paying the tax.[16] In the second half of the century, personal income tax has averaged around 25% of the revenue the government brings in.[17] National insurance contributions, now in effect a second income tax, add around another 18%.[18]

We are so used to income tax that we take it for granted. The vehemence of its Victorian opponents seems naïve, if not strange. And yet, their preferred tax system was surprisingly similar to what is often recommended by both libertarian and progressive policy wonks. Focus taxes on consumption – particularly on luxuries – and land. We did not decide to tax income because we thought it was wise, but because we became addicted to its large revenues. It is not impossible to argue that income tax has been a 200-year mistake.

Incentives matter. The window tax led to windows being blocked up, tax deductions for outfits so long as they were "so outrageous they could not possibly be worn on the street"[19] to ABBA's style of costume. It seems strange, then, that we have based much of our tax system on taxing the one thing we want more of: work.

In the short term, few will change their working habits if their tax bill increases by a few per cent. In the long term, cultural norms change and adapt. In the 1950s, workers in France and Germany worked significantly longer hours than those in America. Over the course of the 1970s, this reversed.[20] Nobel laureate economist Edward Prescott argues that almost all this change can be accounted for by the structure of the tax system.[21] While the US lowered its marginal tax rates, France and Germany kept theirs high.

Personal taxation and welfare benefits are two sides of the same coin. You cannot work out the effect of one without considering the impact of the other – often quite literally, as in the case of tax credits, which are run out of HMRC.

As Beveridge knew, work is the ultimate form of welfare. 'Idleness' is not an evil just because it makes people poor, but because it leads to increased depression, crime and broken families. The only sustainable means to get people out of poverty is to give them the self-respect of a real job.

Both our tax and welfare systems act in too many ways to discourage work. The young find themselves paying for their grandparents' pension, while the still healthy are encouraged to spend a third of their life in retirement. We want companies to implement flexible working so that parents can better juggle work with family, and then put in place decidedly inflexible regulations. An increasing number of the middle class find themselves dragged into paying a higher rate originally intended for the very richest.

Even worse, for those less well off, we both start taxing them as soon as they start work and simultaneously start withdrawing their benefits. Up until the welfare reforms introduced by Iain Duncan Smith, this could mean someone facing an implicit marginal tax rate of anything up to 98%. Is it any surprise that some people would choose not to work more when they are only better off to the tune of 2p in the pound?

The Coalition government's Universal Credit reforms aim to eliminate the very worst of these perverse incentives, but the need for a withdrawal rate which makes this Universal Credit affordable will still lead to many of the poorest earners facing a marginal tax rate of 76%.

The problems associated with our welfare state and the way it is funded are, therefore, clear. Perverse incentives are created by interactions of taxes and benefit withdrawal. There's a high degree of churn, whereby people are highly taxed only to receive their own money back. The state has allowed too many to choose welfare over work, and the lack of a contributory principle means that, while some are seen to get 'something for nothing', others who feel they have contributed receive 'nothing for something' – meagre out-of-work benefits.

What can be done? The ideal tax and welfare system would be simple, predictable, integrated and flexible, and encourage work. There's scope over time for tax reform, swapping taxes on work for taxes on consumption. We could broaden the base for VAT, and increase the tax incentives for savings. Merging income tax with national insurance would be a good step in showing that the contributory function of the welfare state has ceased to exist, and would likely create the political pressure over time for lower marginal tax rates.

In purer welfare terms, the introduction of Universal Credit, integrating benefits together, affords us the chance to make the whole welfare system more pro-work. As the rollout of Universal Credit has suggested, this is easier said in theory than implemented in practice, but the long-term aim should be to bring together as many existing benefits as possible and create a system whereby an individual is in either the tax system or the benefit system, but not both.

Such reforms could easily take decades to put into place, however, and even then would not be a panacea. In reality, one of the great problems associated with the welfare state is its impersonal attempt to try to deal with very personal circumstances. There would still need to be robust workfare aspects and intensive help for the most difficult cases, optimally financed and delivered at a local level. More charitable and voluntary sector provision should be encouraged. And there would still be a requirement, obviously, for provision for those unable to work due to disability. Other areas, such as the problems associated with housing costs and providing for childcare, can only really be effectively delivered through supply-side reforms in the form of more liberalised planning and a deregulated child-minding sector.

All these challenges must be addressed if we are to get back to Beveridge's ideal of a minimum safety net, with strong work incentives and self-provision. There are some smaller things, however, which could be done now to express the direction of travel.

Over the decades, the various tax thresholds have failed to keep up with increases in average earnings. This has gradually ensured that many of us pay a greater proportion of our earnings to the state, facing higher marginal tax rates, and that more people are dragged into the upper tax brackets. The Coalition government have helped halt this for low earners through their significant increases in the personal allowance. But, compared with earnings growth, the level at which individuals start paying the higher rate of income tax at a marginal rate of 40% has fallen significantly.

From the beginning, income tax was a progressive tax, beginning at 2 pennies in the pound for incomes over £60, and increasing to 2 shillings in the pound for incomes over £200, a 10% rate. Given contemporary incomes, this meant that only high income earners paid any income tax at all, and the higher rate was reserved for the very rich. In 1909, Lloyd George introduced a 'supertax', double the standard rate at 7.5%, and targeted at the very rich, those with incomes above £5,000. That is the equivalent of around £500,000 today, or seventy times average earnings at the time.[22]

An employee working for four days a week on the minimum wage would already be liable for the basic rate of income tax, and the higher rate is increasingly becoming a tax faced by those at the height of their career or living in the South East. Income tends to peak when you are in your forties, and, similarly, the limits make no allowances for regional variation in wages and living costs. There is no equivalent to London weighting for taxation. In April 2013, median full-time annual gross earnings in London were around £35,000.[23]

In the longer term, to protect all taxpayers and to prevent the most pernicious effects of fiscal drag, we should change the default baselines so that income tax and national insurance thresholds automatically go up with inflation or average earnings, whichever is higher. The government could override this if it needed to, but it would have to bring the matter to a vote. This would prevent taxpayers facing higher and higher marginal rates, with all the negative incentives this brings.

Second, we need to get more creative in terms of the incentives we use to encourage work other than direct subsidies. Welfare experts often talk of an 'iron triangle'. If you want to reduce the expense of the benefits bill, you either have to decrease the level for the very poorest, or withdraw it faster as those claimants get a job, discouraging work. Obviously, neither of those alternatives, or simply spending an ever greater amount on welfare, is ideal.

There is a way to break out of the iron triangle, but this would take us beyond the scope of welfare policy, narrowly defined. The level of income replacement benefits cannot be set without regard for the cost of attaining a basic standard of living. The British welfare system reflects this: housing benefit rates have long been pegged to rent levels, and direct childcare subsidies are paid as a reimbursement of actual expenses, which is why they follow childcare costs. Energy and food prices have no direct influence on benefit rates, but it is difficult to imagine that they do not affect the rate-setting process at all. At least in the UK, the cost of these items is not simply determined by the market, but to a very large extent by government policies – planning laws, regulation of childcare providers, green energy obligations, agricultural protectionism and so on. If we implemented serious supply-side reforms, welfare benefits could be cut *without* lowering the recipients' standard of living.[24]

But we should also look at other ways to encourage work – while making sure that the system is not cruel to those who have simply been unlucky.

For example, we could revive Beveridge's contributory principle for young people. Young individuals who have not yet paid national insurance contributions for a certain period, five years say, could receive their unemployment benefit in the form of a repayable loan. An unemployed teenager would still receive the same amount of cash as now, for example, but they would be expected to repay the value once in work. Turning an entitlement into a loan would mean that people would still be supported while out of work, but would have an additional incentive to find work rather than allow the debt to build up.

Like tuition fee repayment, this would not mean huge repayments, and the repayments required would be tapered by income through the Universal Credit system to ensure that it was always better to work. It would only actually reduce the recipient's take-home income after they were earning enough to be out of the territory of other benefits.

It cannot be right that people can be stuck on unemployment benefits for many years, and never reach a point where they have contributed enough to balance out the debt to the taxpayer that they have incurred. Even if someone were unfortunate enough to be out of work for the entire seven years between 18 and 25, the total sum repayable would be £20,475 – considerably less than the tuition fees loan repayable by many of his or her peers.

The flip side of this is that we could do more to reward those who have a long record of contribution. As a rule of thumb, five years of contribution should mean six months of unconditional unemployment benefit, ten years a year, and twenty years two years. This would give a much fairer deal to people who unexpectedly lose their job later in life, having already paid considerable sums in tax and national insurance.

This would also fulfil Beveridge's tough-minded vision. Beveridge anticipated the modern trend towards greater conditionality and was decidedly radical on benefits for young people. He recommended that there be no unconditional benefit whatsoever for 'boys and girls', and that any period spent out of work should be an opportunity for further compulsory training.

What Beveridge did not foresee was the connection between childcare and work. In the twenty-first century, working is likely to become ever more flexible –as a result of both technology and parents' demand for a better balance between home and work life. At present, government is hurting, not helping, this trend. Expensive over-regulation is raising the price of childcare, while too much of the burden of administering maternity and paternity pay is being placed upon employers. It would be better to replace maternity and paternity pay with a flat 'Baby Bonus', paid directly from the government. Mothers and fathers would then be given an entitlement to unpaid leave, and employers could, as now, top this up if they desired.

These measures, on top of the medium to long-term ambitions outlined earlier, would go some way to reverse some of the damaging trends of the welfare state since Beveridge's report.

But for policy makers, it's not enough to remedy current problems. You have to anticipate future challenges.

After all, what is the point of encouraging work if robots are about to take all the jobs anyway? Welfare isn't just about work, some argue, but our only chance to patch over a growing inequality that threatens to tear our society apart.

One Nation

Inequality is falling. For the first time since the Industrial Revolution, the take-up of market ideas in the emerging world has led to developing nations catching up faster than the Western world can extend its lead. This is true on dry statistical grounds – the Gini index of world inequality seems to have finally reached a turning point in the last twenty years[25] – but far more revealing is the drop in poverty. Income in sub-Saharan Africa has climbed by two-thirds since 1998, from $1,300 to $2,200. Since 1960, the lifespan for women has gone up from forty-one to fifty-seven years. On current trends, Bill Gates predicts that in twenty years child mortality in the developing world should have reached American or British levels from 1980, fifteen deaths in every 1,000 births. "By 2035", he argues, "there will be almost no poor countries left in the world."[26]

But, while the overall news on the world scene is bright, many have darker fears about inequality within countries. The rewards from globalisation are clear for the poorest in the developing world, and the rich in the developed, but what about the middle? Will a new endless supply of cheap labour undercut living standards for families in the West? Are we seeing a hollowed-out middle class, as technology automates away services jobs? Are the rewards from growth increasingly going to the '1%', while median incomes stagnate? Are we in a 'cost of living crisis' that stretches back not just four years, but four decades?

When faced with a problem, it is important to diagnose the causes properly. Some have blamed the slowdown in ordinary incomes on predatory companies, taking advantage of a workforce no longer protected by heavy unionisation. This just doesn't seem to match the data. In both Britain and America, workers are still being paid broadly the amount of value they create for their employer, their marginal productivity.[27] Unfortunately, two roughly equal effects have reduced take-home pay family for the average family. The first is the increase in pension costs and the tax employers have to pay on jobs. The second effect is potentially more worrying. While employees are being paid for the value they produce, this productivity is increasingly diverging.

It has long been recognised that technology and globalisation act as a multiplier for the skilled and talented. It took Enid Blyton 700 books to achieve her half billion in book sales – J. K. Rowling got there with seven. Wages for global 'superstars', from university professors to actual film stars, have rocketed.

But this doesn't just impact the top 1% or 0.1%. Technological change disproportionately benefits the talented and the educated right across the population. Highly skilled programmers can look forward to well-paid careers for decades to come, while checkout workers are already being replaced.

The obvious response is to redouble our efforts to improve the skills of everyone, reforming our education system to raise standards, in particular in maths, science and IT. The idea that the future is predetermined against many people, and that we should just give up on them by guaranteeing them comfortable future incomes without working, is far too pessimistic.

But it would be equally overly Panglossian to predict that even the best education system in the world can perfectly equalise everyone's talents. It is probably inevitable that, statistically at least, income inequality will rise in future decades.

This isn't quite as bad as it sounds. Despite frequent paranoia, there is relatively little evidence that increased wealth allows the rich to buy influence at elections.[28] Moreover, consumption inequality – what people actually spend – is much more equal than income.

In recent years, a trope has developed that increased national growth is no longer making many of us any happier, while inequality makes us all more stressed as we compete in an endless rat race.

The reverse is closer to the truth. As you would intuitively expect, an extra £100 is worth far more to the poor than the rich. Nevertheless, if there is a limit on how happy extra money can make us, we have yet to reach it. Our best data suggests that every doubling of income increases satisfaction with our lives by 0.34 of a standard deviation compared with the rest of the population.[29]

By contrast, greater welfare spending has no statistical effect on happiness, even for the unemployed.[30] The self-respect of having a job is far more important than crude redistribution. Inequality seems to have no independent effect on happiness – unless, somewhat perversely, you are in a culture that already worries about it. In cultures like the US, which believe in the potential of meritocracy, inequality has no effect on the happiness of the poor. The reverse is true in Europe.

All in all, income inequality is a very poor measure of the kinds of poverty we care most about. Growth has brought equality in nearly all the dimensions that truly matter: shelter, warmth, clothes, nutrition, free time, information, technology and entertainment. Twenty years ago, only a billionaire would have been able to afford the power of a smartphone. Soon, a ten-year-old will be able to. Only a few could go to the opera in the eighteenth century – everyone gets to see a Hollywood blockbuster. Both the poor and the rich pay the same proportion of their income to use Google: nothing. One study by William Nordhaus suggests that inventors only capture 2.2% of the value they create for wider society.[31] Future innovation is likely to follow the same trend – for a few years available to only the few, before being rapidly commoditised for everyone else.

French economist Thomas Piketty has argued that we face a new era of inequality in wealth. Under his theory, the rate of return on capital is likely in the twenty-first century to significantly exceed the growth of wages. Capital owners will gradually take over an ever larger part of the economy.

This might have been true in the pre-modern economy. Before the Industrial Revolution, much wealth came from inherited land rather than business innovation and risk taking. It is much less clear whether it will be true for the twenty-first century, when many businesses require little more capital than a computer and an internet connection – but, even if it were to be the case, it would mostly present a very good argument for privatisation of social security. If capital grows faster than taxpayer revenue, why not spread a capital-owning democracy as far as possible?

What really offends most people is not inequality per se. As is often noted, few really begrudge J. K. Rowling or David Beckham or Bill Gates their riches. Most people don't even agree with the moral philosophers who argue that wealth created by undeserved 'luck' is illegitimate. Few complain about the inequality caused by the National Lottery.

What really matters is fairness. Ultimately, fairness can't be decided simply by looking at the division of the pie. We have to drill down into the mechanisms on a case-by-case basis.

Unfair inequality does exist – but, unfortunately, much of it is ultimately caused by government. It is government, not markets, that subsidises too-big-to-fail banks, allowing such high bonuses. It is government that pays the public sector more than the private, and drives up wages by excessive occupational licensing. Regulation, hidden taxes and minimum prices drive up the cost of basic goods for the poor, such as food, energy and childcare. The service you receive from a Pizza Express or Odeon is pretty much the same everywhere – it is public services that show such a wide diversity in quality across the nation. Even Piketty's wealth inequality, once you look at the numbers, is largely driven by increasing property wealth, often the result of government planning laws.

If we want to reduce inequality and create a true one nation, this is the best place to start. Even the believers in price fixing, endless subsidies and wage restrictions don't pretend that there is no possibility of negative side effects. By contrast, a free enterprise approach to tackling inequality is almost entirely win-win. It increases productivity and reduces the cost of living.

The most important inequality of all comes from employment. If you want to look at a truly unequal economy, look at Spain. Its excessive system of labour market regulation has created a two-tier economy, split between those in secure jobs and those left without. Combined with the disaster of the Eurozone, it has created an unemployment rate of 26% – and, at one point, 56% for the under-25s.[32]

One study by the Centre for Economic Performance found that five years after a divorce or bereavement, most people's reported life satisfaction had returned to its pre-tragedy level. By contrast, we never seem to adapt to unemployment. Five years later, it stung almost the same as in the first year.[33] Leaving someone trapped on a lifetime of benefits is about the cruellest thing you can do.

Will the coming wave of technological advances massively increase unemployment, especially for those in the middle? In their book *Race against The Machine*,[34] Erik Brynjolfsson and Andrew McAfee argue that computer-based technology is rendering many previous low-level service jobs obsolete. It's easy to think of examples. Supermarket staff have been replaced by self-service checkout machines and airline check-in attendants by self-login computers. In future, even the taxi driver may soon be put out of work by the driverless car.

In the very long run, the prospect of continued 'technological unemployment' is unlikely. Nobody can predict the new jobs, just as nobody can predict what companies will be started in thirty years. However, as long as we still prefer the human touch over a machine, some kinds of employment are unlikely to go away. Even when a train or bus can drive itself, there will still be a place for a guard to answer passenger questions or help out in an emergency. Is it such a bad thing that many of the most boring or dangerous jobs are being replaced by machines? In the very worst-case scenario, we might simply finally reach the world predicted by Keynes in *Economic Possibilities for our Grandchildren* of ever-decreasing working hours.

Even in the short term, the problem can be overstated. Labour-saving technologies might destroy some roles, but they also create demand for new products and services. The immediate effect of automatic checkouts may be that a lot of cashiers lose their jobs, but, in order to evaluate the full effect, we need to look a bit further. Supermarkets would not install this technology if it were not cost-saving, and, in a competitive retail sector, those costs will ultimately be passed on to consumers in the form of lower prices. Consumers will effectively be richer, and spend their effective extra income in other sectors, thereby creating new jobs elsewhere in the economy.

This is not just grey theory. Empirically, we do observe that some of the most productive, technology-intensive economies, such as Switzerland, also display some of the lowest unemployment rates. Technology often determines the composition, but not the level, of employment.

However, it is certainly possible that we are entering a more dynamic era with greater industrial upheaval. Certainly, the lifespan of companies is shrinking. The pessimists therefore say that we should be more accepting of people being paid not to work and of the government taking a strongly redistributive outlook – both to prevent high levels of inequality and to provide a higher minimum level of income, given the lack of job opportunities. But the idea that any problems can be effectively extinguished, without different negative consequences, by simply giving higher levels of unconditional welfare is at odds with historical experience.

Instead, we need to do more to make sure that people aren't condemned to a life on benefits rather than starting out again in a new career, as happened for many in the 1980s. Allowing the erosion of skills through what economists call 'hysteresis' – being out of the labour market for a sustained period – causes lack of self-esteem, unhappiness, lower earnings potential and a sense of powerlessness. The welfare system should aim to get individuals back into the labour market sooner rather than later.

Both welfare and labour market regulations have to be more flexible, too. Technological change, with more cheaply produced machine products and services, is likely to mean more enterprises, with many self-employed. More individuals are likely to operate what are described as 'portfolio careers', less attached to any single firm, often learning across their working lives, and doing bits and pieces – flexibly and independently. The idea of the 'job for life' and employer-led benefits, already dwindling, may not really exist.

Welfare provision therefore has to be available for those who move in and out of the labour market on a frequent basis. Too often the application process or delay in receipt of benefits in the result of losing an uncertain job deters individuals from taking up the job in the first place. In this changing world, we cannot afford for this to be the case. It's vital, too, that employment regulations maximise the possibility of obtaining work or experience in order to stay linked to the labour market. At the same time, we also have to make it easier for individuals to physically move across the country in search of work – a process again not helped by our planning regulations.

It's difficult to know exactly what impacts technological change will have, though. Thankfully, making the welfare, tax and employment markets more flexible and work-oriented would be a beneficial thing to do irrespective of the scale of disruption.

Eventually, however, we all do have to stop working. While political pressure focuses on unemployment and poverty-related benefit costs, by far the biggest component of the welfare bill comes from provisions for pensioners, and this is only going to become a more significant issue in the coming decades.

Ageing Britain

The Industrial Revolution brought not just more wealth, but more time. Higher standards of living, improved sanitation and more effective medicine all helped children survive through to maturity, reduce infectious disease and keep Britons living longer. At the beginning of the nineteenth century, average life expectancy in Britain was around forty years. We now live, on average, twice as long as that. To begin with, improvements in the Victorian era came from improving the chances of surviving till adulthood. Over the second half of the twentieth century, however, ages at the upper end finally began to climb. If you retired at the turn of the millennium, you could expect to live another seventeen years, five years longer than someone retiring in 1950.

Across the world, the upper end of average life expectancy has improved at a remarkably constant rate of three months per year for more than a century. Since 1950 the number of people living to 100 has doubled each decade.[35] Despite this steady increase, and the decreasing proportion of society engaged in hard manual labour, for a hundred years the state pension age remained frozen at sixty-five or less.

As far as we can predict, average ages will continue to rise for the foreseeable future. The ONS's central projection is for future life expectancy at age sixty-five to increase an extra five to six years over the next half century.[36] While we may eventually hit a limit – humans seem to hit a natural genetic barrier at around 110[37] – at this pace we should not hit it until at least the next century.

This ageing of our society will have at least three large effects. The first is that worldwide pension ages will continue to creep up, and those who can will work for longer. In Britain, this has already been largely accepted. The current government's decision to automatically link retirement ages to life expectancy implies that a new worker can expect to work until their seventieth birthday. More than a hundred years after Bismarck set the first state pension age at seventy, we will have come largely full circle.

Second, even given the higher retirement age, the aged population has the potential to put considerable stress on the public finances. This will be not so much because of the direct higher costs of pensions as because of the increased strain placed on health and social care. The only way to afford this will be more efficient and innovative public services.

Finally, an ageing population will require us all to save more for our retirement. The state pension should be seen as a starting point, a minimum for us all to build on. It is neither affordable nor necessary for governments to do our savings for us. This is a significant task. Nineteen per cent of Britons have no savings at all at the moment, while only 12% have more than £50,000.[38]

While these changes may be dramatic, they are not unprecedented. Across our history, our ideas of and expectations for retirement have inevitably evolved as lifespans lengthened. The expectation that healthy men should abruptly retire from work at a given age is largely a twentieth century idea. As late as 1875, a significant proportion of British males over the age of sixty-five were still in work.

Pensions, instead, were intended for the widowed, the extremely poor or those too ill to work. While the concept of a pension goes back at least as far as the Roman Empire, up until the nineteenth century they were reserved for a small group of retired soldiers, clergymen and guild members. For those without a pension who were too ill to work there was, instead, private charity, or, from 1600, the Elizabethan Poor Law and outdoor relief.

In the Victorian era, the idea of a pension become much more widespread, although it was then largely seen as a matter for private savings. The move to an industry economy, increased life expectancy, greater individual wealth, and the tightening of the Poor Law in the 1830s all led to far higher private savings. The developments of modern actuarial and financial techniques allowed the spread of pooled life insurance schemes, often delivered through guilds or the increasingly popular friendly societies. By the end of the century, the largest firms were offering pensions to their employees, and civil servants were increasingly enjoying their own pensions. Further increases in life expectancy, however, were putting real pressure on the finances of friendly societies, while there were always many who were too poor to save, and who fell through the gaps in the system. Pressure began to grow for the state to take over.

The international template for state pensions came from conservative Otto von Bismarck's Germany in 1889. Much like Disraeli's extension of the franchise in 1867, Bismarck believed in buying off the demands of the left to support his greater aims. Introducing a state pension would "engender in the great mass of the unpropertied the conservative state of mind that springs from the feeling of entitlement to a pension". Nevertheless, the scheme was at first relatively modest: set at around 20% of average pay, excluding agricultural works and only claimable from the age of seventy.

The idea of a state pension had been discussed in Britain even before this, with a Select Committee in 1885 concluding that a national pooled savings system was financially unviable. Over the next few decades, the issue continued its political prominence, with politicians such as Joseph Chamberlain agonising over the dilemma between an expensive, universal scheme and the damage to self-help and savings from a more limited means-tested pension.

In the end, the Liberal Party in 1908 decided to go for a limited non-contributory system. It would pay up to five shillings a week to those over seventy who earned less than £31 and ten shillings a year – the equivalent of £20 and £2,700, respectively, in today's money. The principal effect of the pension was to remove the perceived stigma of poor relief, and extend the coverage of those who qualified.

From the start, this pension was recognised as being, at most, an experimental beginning. In 1926, it was augmented by a second contributory system. The Old Age, Widows and Orphans Contributory Act extended the national insurance system, creating a new pension which started at age sixty-five for men and sixty for women. This system was still far from comprehensive: it was only compulsory for manual workers, and excluded those with higher incomes.

Unfortunately, neither system really paid out enough to live off on its own. Beveridge's 1942 report suggested their replacement by a universal, fully contributory scheme. He proposed a fully funded scheme, paying out a flat-rate income high enough to avoid poverty. In the end, this proved too expensive: instead, it was decided that the 1946 National Insurance Act would introduce a 'pay-as-you-go' system. In terms of pension reform, Beveridge was not a 'British Bismarck', though. Unlike his more authoritarian-minded continental counterpart, Beveridge appreciated the value of private initiative in this area, and sought to minimise the 'crowding-out effect'.

Nor did the system ever really pay out a flat rate. From the beginning, the system was augmented with other means-tested benefits, from National Assistance at its origins to Pension Credit in the New Labour years. At the same time, there was continual pressure to move to a more European system in which the state pension would act more like an occupational pension, paying out a given proportion of earnings. In 1961, Macmillan's government introduced a second earnings-related pension scheme, originally known as the Graduated Retirement Benefit. While this was to continue to evolve, governments repeatedly found that a true social insurance scheme was too expensive.

In this sense, the 1960s reforms gave the British pension system a more Bismarckian feel. However, in line with Beveridge's aim of preserving private initiative, a concept that set the British system apart from its Continental European equivalents was introduced in parallel: contracting out. Essentially, this meant that those who were already part of a private, savings-based pension plan, for example through their workplace, were not required to join the new earnings-related state pension scheme. Nor did they have to pay the concomitant national insurance rate that financed this pension. Throughout the post-war period, the UK gave people the opportunity to opt out of a part of the state pension, receive national insurance rebates equivalent to the pension entitlements foregone, and use those rebates to build up a private pension fund instead.[39] Britain thus retained elements of a private, savings-based system, while most of the developed world adopted pure public pay-as-you-go systems. This tradition has gradually been eroded over time, but it could be revived once more. Savings are currently far too low, but, as a legacy of the contracting-out policy, at least a 'savings infrastructure' is still in place.

By the 1990s, it was becoming clear internationally that public pension systems needed reform. An influential World Bank report in 1994, "Averting the Old Age Crisis", argued that pay-as-you-go pensions systems had become unaffordable, and that they should be replaced by a three-pronged system: a limited, universal system to reduce poverty; mandatory private savings to create a funded system; and then a third voluntary saving system on top of this.

This is largely the approach that Britain has chosen to take. The first significant reform came in 1995, when it was decided that between 2010 and 2020 the state pension age should be gradually equalised between men and women. In 2002, Labour initiated a Pensions Commission led by Adair Turner to review the system. It concluded that the state pension age should rise to 68 – enough to slow the growth of pensions spending, but not fully offset it. Labour went on to legislate for this in 2007. In addition, to increase private savings, Labour legislated in 2008 for workers to be automatically enrolled in a pension scheme – although they could still choose to opt out.

Under the Coalition, the increase in the state pension age has been accelerated and is now linked automatically to increases in life expectancy. At the same time, the Coalition plans to merge the two major components of the state pension into a single-tier pension from 2016. This will be set at just above the basic level of means-tested support, and will increase from then on at least in line with earnings.

These are good first steps, though the government has cancelled out some of the long-term savings brought about by the planned increases to the retirement age because of introducing the triple-lock state pension guarantee. This will see it rise every year in line with wages or with prices or by 2.5%, whichever is highest. It seems likely, then, that in future we will see further increases in the state pension age brought forward, as governments seek to grapple with their long-term pay-as-you-go liabilities.

In this regard, the case for auxiliary non-means-tested pensioner benefits such as the winter fuel allowance, free TV licences and bus passes is looking decidedly weak. This is particularly true given the increased generosity of the state pension. It seems likely that these additional benefits will eventually be abolished, or at the very least rolled into the state pension, which would enjoy a one-time uplift.

In the grand scheme of things, these are small-fry measures, however. What is ultimately required are measures to encourage us both to work for longer and to save more. This is the only way to prevent suffocating increases in tax rates to maintain our current pay-as-you-go health and pension systems.

The employment rate among men aged between fifty-five and fifty-nine decreased from over 90% to less than 70% between 1968 and the end of the 1990s, and, despite increasing to about 80% by 2008, is still below the level seen nearly four decades ago.[40] This is a huge waste, especially given the rise in 'healthy' life expectancy. Aside from the economic costs, recent research indicates that being retired decreases physical, mental and self-assessed health. The adverse effects increase as the number of years spent in retirement increases.[41] The key result suggests that being retired reduces the chance of being in excellent or very good self-assessed health by 40%. This implies that remaining economically active is not just good for the public finances, but for maintaining our individual health – a win-win, given the future strains likely to be imposed on the NHS by ageing.

It has generally been recognised that we need more of a savings culture in the UK. This has been undermined by a dysfunctional savings industry and conflicting government policies. As Michael Johnson's extensive work for the Centre for Policy Studies has shown, the UK's household savings rate is extremely low. It is a huge test of both policy and the behaviour of individuals as to whether this can be substantially increased. The 2014 Budget began what looks like a process of major reform of pensions by reducing the tax rate on pension withdrawals after the age of fifty-five and abolishing the need to buy an annuity. This will give savers much more flexibility to use their money as they see fit.

The merging of cash and stocks and shares ISAs, and the increased tax-free limit for ISAs, are further evidence of how much the government believes more flexibility for savers is key to regenerating a savings culture. This suggests that Johnson's idea of allocating a Super ISA account at birth with a default provider (like the Post Office), identified by a national insurance number, could serve as a long-term general and retirement savings vehicle. His idea for ISAs to be linked to future NEST accounts (to become Super ISAs) should also be seriously considered.

The crux of the matter is that we simply have to save more. Nowhere is this more true than in social care.

The Social Care Market

Who really saves for their elderly care? In a 2008 survey, 3% of people claimed that they were already saving for their long-term care, 32% that they had plans to do so, and 64% that they had not. For people aged between sixteen and thirty-five, 73% claimed that they had no plans to pay for their future social care – an unsurprising yet worrying proportion.

Adult social care has effectively operated as a market since the 1980s, which saw an expansion in the number of private care homes. The care sector is currently estimated by the Department of Health to be worth around £23 billion. However, the bewildering complexity of the system has led to inefficiencies – making it difficult for the market to anticipate and react properly to consumer demand. This is not only detrimental to individuals receiving care, but to the taxpayers on whom much of the cost of social care falls.

The future of social care presently lies in personalisation, especially with the current rollout of personal budgets in social care. Setting aside the question of funding for the time being, for personalisation to work there must be a sophisticated and diverse market available for care services, which will allow users genuine choice. Though a distinction should be drawn between personalisation and personal budgets, it is this individual control over care that will help drive market development.

Former health minister Lord Warner highlights the potential that efficiently delivered social care has to save money for the NHS – claiming that an eighty-year-old in hospital costs around £3,000 per week, whereas in a medically supervised nursing home the figure would be around £1,000 per week.[42] Since 2005, emergency admissions for people aged over eighty-five have increased by 48% – something that is preventable by effective community or home-based care.[43]

Local authorities faced with budget difficulties all too often see care services as low-hanging fruit for cuts, as they are much less visible than libraries or potholes. Authorities are responsible for interpreting whether or not a charge is appropriate for the care services that they provide. This generally takes the form of a means test – though the discretionary nature has led to a patchwork system, with different charges and levels of eligibility depending on which authority an individual lives in. For example, it is estimated that 72% of councils now only offer homecare services to people with needs rated as 'substantial' or 'critical'.[44]

In Germany, 90% of the population are covered by compulsory long-term care insurance, introduced in 1994–1995 as a result of financial pressures on Länder. A significant goal for this reform was to reduce the number of people relying on social assistance.

Here, too, cash payments in lieu of professional services are also popular, and sustain informal care-giving. Indeed, in Germany the cost of cash payments is around half that of professional services – though individuals are also able to tailor their own mixture of the two. The comparatively low cost of these cash payments is incredibly useful in keeping the overall cost of the system down – and those receiving them are required to request advice from a professional care service to ensure quality of care.

In 2007, people who need considerable care (care level I) received €384 per month, those in need of intensive care (care level II) €921, and people in need of highly intensive care (care level III) €1,432 per month.

By contrast, with direct cash payments people at care level I received €205, at care level II €410, and people at care level III €665 per month.

For nursing home care, the tariffs were set at €1,023, €1,279 and €1,432 respectively. German legislation mandates that the insurance system should support patients being cared for at home over residential care.

Perhaps surprisingly, then, these lump sum transfers are opted for by nearly half of the 1,977,296 people receiving care benefits.

Forty-nine per cent chose the cash, 27.3% nursing home care, 10.3% some combination of cash and services, and 8.6% only in-kind services. The rest is accounted for by institutional care for the disabled (3.2%), day/night care (0.7%), respite care (0.5%) and short-term care (0.5%).[45]

German federal law stimulates market development and competition. Insurance funds negotiate and purchase care from various providers for domiciliary and institutional care services. Private and charitable organisations, under federal law, are given preference over public providers.[46] This encourages a broader range of competing providers, driving down prices.

Talking about this in purely economic terms ignores the greatest advantage of all – many people fundamentally want to be looked after at home, by people they know and trust. This is why we already see such a huge amount of informal care – family members feel a sense of duty, which should be both applauded and supported. Making this a viable alternative to residential care, through direct payments, will be socially as well as economically beneficial. Though Britain does not have the same cultural inclination as many other countries – where one sees several generations of one family living under the same roof – where people are willing to do this it should be encouraged by the government.

New providers need to enter the market to stimulate innovation, and failed providers must leave. The example of Southern Cross is instructive: a failed model of care home ownership led to the collapse of the business. However, the vast majority of Southern Cross homes were transferred to alternative operators in 2011, securing a continuity of provision without the need for a taxpayer bailout. This shows that the market can also work to insure against failure – even on the massive scale of Southern Cross – as long as there are enough alternative providers competing for the business. The nature of the business encourages service continuity, as failing care homes lose considerable value if they are not sold as a going concern. This is one example of an effective commercial incentive for providers to offload unsuccessful homes to alternative providers when suffering financial difficulties.

At present, direct control from local authorities means that providers are too often reliant on a single customer for their services, lessening the power of competition. A 2004 market survey suggested that 60% of independent providers saw more than 75% of their business come from local authorities, and that 15% had local authorities as their only customers.[47] Increasing the control that individuals have over their care budgets will stimulate greater competition among providers.

At present the social care system is poorly understood, and not simply on account of its complexity. For many people, an understanding of how their care may or may not be funded comes only when they begin to need it, frequently providing a nasty financial shock. Even fewer people have made appropriate provision earlier in their life to cover future care costs.

We need to do more to unleash a savings culture for care. One possibility would be the creation of a 'Care ISA', a tax-free investment much like an ISA. This would work like a regular ISA, except that the maximum investment could be far larger, to the value of the cap on care costs announced by the government of £72,000. Access to the ISA could then only be spent on care services within a family. Clearly, there would need to be registered care services or providers who could then access funds within the ISA, ensuring that the system could not be open to abuse. Above all, it must be clear that money saved is money for care and nothing else.

Possibly returns on investment could be index-linked to the age of the participant, similarly to life insurance maturity. Perhaps most importantly, a growth in Care ISAs would ensure that an insurance market was able to grow effectively in the knowledge that a care savings culture had finally been created – indeed, possession of a Care ISA might become a prerequisite for accessing care insurance.

Finally, governments have to be much clearer on how the funding model for social care will operate in practice. Two of the key reasons given by insurers and annuities providers for low take-up in this area are uncertainty and the belief that the state provides care free of charge. In order for there to be any chance that the new Dilnot cost cap of £72,000 will generate any sort of meaningful market for insurance or care-linked savings products (and this is highly doubtful), the public must be made aware that the cap excludes living or hotel costs, and that it is not a cap on actual spend. Rather, it is based on what a local authority would spend if the individual were eligible for support in the means test. This is significant, because it means that many going into care in the South East will still pay an extremely high proportion of the costs that they would have paid prior to the cost cap being introduced.

THE FREE ENTERPRISE MANIFESTO – TAXATION AND WELFARE:

1) We should automatically increase tax thresholds with the higher of inflation or average earnings.
2) We should convert Jobseekers' Allowance into a repayable loan for those under twenty-five without a long record of national insurance contributions. Those over twenty-five should get more time to find work, depending on their record.
3) We should replace maternity and paternity pay with a flat Baby Bonus paid out directly by the government.
4) We should create Care ISAs, a new tax-free investment vehicle to encourage us all to save more for our own social care. Individuals should be given the choice of taking a cash payment for their social care.

PART II

Market

The Innovation Economy

Many worry that we have entered a 'new normal' of low productivity, or that our economy has become dangerously unbalanced. However, there are many reasons to be optimistic about the future. As a creative and high-skilled economy, we are well placed to benefit from future technology. Attempts to plan for this future or pick winners are likely to prove counter-productive, restricting the competition that is the real driver of increased productivity. Unfortunately, government regulation has created inefficient oligopolies in too many sectors across our economy, including banking, utilities and the media. The most effective competition comes from new entrants, and it is still too hard to start and grow a new business in Britain.

The Productivity Puzzle

The immediate decades after the war were a golden era for much of the Western world. For Britain, however, this was always slightly tinged by our relative underperformance. The US and Continental Europe were increasingly leaving us behind. British workers, it seemed, just weren't as efficient.

In 1978, measured in real terms, British workers produced 11% less than the Germans, 19% less than the Austrians, 20% less than the French and a colossal 43% less than the Americans.

Then Margaret Thatcher happened. A decade of tax cuts, privatisations and market-based reforms changed the nature of the economy. British productivity growth began to accelerate, and we started to catch up. By 2007 we were 9% more efficient than the Germans, 2% more efficient than the French, just 3% behind the Austrians and 21% behind the US.[1]

In the wake of the financial crisis, British productivity once again began to disappoint. The financial system suffered just as great a shock in the US as in the UK, but it was Britain that was to see productivity stagnate and even fall over the next few years. Economists began to wonder just how much of the improvement of the so-called 'Great Moderation' period had been real.

Many of the old complaints about the British economy became popular again. We didn't invest enough in either the public or the private sector. Our managers were too short-sighted, focused on the next quarter's stock price, rather than the long-term interests of company and community. We needed to learn from continental countries such as Germany. Management, government and trade unions should work together, rather than ceaselessly fight. Our economy was hopelessly unbalanced, too reliant on financial services in general and London in particular. We no longer 'made things', and had allowed our manufacturing sector to shrink. We were too naive, allowing foreign companies to buy up historic British brands like Cadbury's or build crucial infrastructure such as our power stations. The only solution was a new generation of activist industrial policy: government investment banks, subsidies for manufacturing and increased private–public partnerships.

Some on the left have gone even further than this. The British economy is broken, they argue. In too many markets, an ideological mistrust of regulation has led to predatory companies running amok, taking advantage of both customers and their workers. What is needed is for government to once more take a stronger hand, breaking up monopolistic companies wherever possible, and capping or freezing prices wherever not. In their view, the 'neoliberal agenda' never worked. The growth from the Great Moderation period was nothing more than a mirage, a twenty-year bubble brought about by unsustainable financial services and rapidly draining North Sea oil.

Even for many on the right, there were severe worries about the economy's fundamentals. How much had the Thatcher revolution transformed the underlying economy, and how much had we enjoyed a one-off boom from cheap commodities, unsustainable debt and offshoring to the Far East? Were we doomed to a 'new normal' of low growth?

Ultimately, what really makes a difference to our standard of living is productivity, determined by innovations and encouraged by a robust supply side of the economy. In the long term, it determines not just the wealth of our nation as a whole, or the size of the tax revenues our government can safely harvest, but the amount each of us earns in a job.

Very few questions matter more, then, than working out what is going on with productivity. Is our economy broken and unbalanced? Did the Thatcher reforms really make a difference, or only shield our consistent decline? Do we need a new generation of industrial policy? How exactly will we make our living in the future?

A Nation of Shopkeepers

For much of human history, there has been just one career track. For 12,000 years, the vast majority of ordinary families could expect to spend their days farming.

Georgian Britain, however, was different. By 1760, just half of the male labour force is estimated to have worked on the land. Eighty years later, it would be under a third.[2] Stealing Adam Smith's phrase, Napoleon infamously referred to England as a 'nation of shopkeepers'. Britain was a mercantile nation, more interested in trade and commerce than war or land.

Ironically, by the time Napoleon made the jibe, it was already growing less true. The arrival of the Industrial Revolution had turned the nation of shopkeepers into the 'workshop of the world'. By the time of the census in 1841, more people worked in either manufacturing (36%) or services (33%) than in agriculture (22%). By 1901, Britain was arguably the world's first post-agricultural society, with fewer than 10% of its workforce working the land.[3] In the US, by contrast, 38% of the workforce were farmers. Agriculture was not to drop to 10% until half a century later.[4]

This collapse in farming's share of the economy did not happen because agriculture failed. Nor was it simply a matter of Britain outsourcing its food production to other nations. Agriculture shrank because its productivity improved. We could do more for less – and, despite today's concerns about obesity, there really is only so much we can eat. For much of human history, most farm workers could provide just about enough food to feed themselves and their families, and not much more. By 1900, a single farm worker in Britain could feed twenty-five people, and by 2010 two hundred.[5]

The second half of the twentieth century was to see this pattern repeated in manufacturing. In 1951, the proportion employed in manufacturing was identical to that over a century before: 36%. By

2011, this had fallen to just one in eleven people, or 9%. Over four out of five of us now work in some form of services.

Just as with the decline in agriculture, these changes faced resistance from those worried about what would replace the declining industries. Some complained bitterly that British manufacturing had been deliberately undercut by a politics more concerned with protecting the golden goose of the City.

For the most part, however, the decline in manufacturing has been the result of natural economic gravity. Much of it is explained by improving technology. While it has shrunk as a proportion of the economy, the actual amount of goods produced by British manufacturing has continued to increase.

An even larger impact has come from changing consumer demand. We have spent most of the increase in our incomes on increased services rather than manufactured goods. Most people only need one oven, but have considerable scope to expand the number of meals they eat out. Between 1980 and 2008, we spent just 13% of the increase in our incomes on manufactured products.[6]

A final effect came from joining the European Common Market. Victorian economist David Ricardo famously explained the principle of comparative advantage, by pointing out that it was more efficient for Portugal to specialise in wine and Britain in cloth, and trade the difference. If you swap cloth for services, and Portugal and wine for Germany and manufacturing, this is more or less what has happened. Britain has focused on its comparative advantage of services – the nation of shopkeepers, once again – while Germany looked to its traditional strength in manufacturing.

Despite the inevitability of this process, successive generations of politicians sought to hold back the tide through repeated rounds of industrial policy. Unlike short-sighted industry or finance, it was believed, the government could take the long view about manufacturing's importance to Britain's future. If Britain's firms couldn't keep up with efficient foreigners, that was because there were too many of them, creating wasteful competition and repetition.

From the 1930s on, governments reorganised Britain's industries. They 'rationalised' them into new oligopolies, appointed national champions, and, when all else failed, nationalised them. They protected British industries behind trade barriers and gave them a helping hand with subsidies. New government departments and QUANGOs were created to do what the market could not. The 1945 Industrial and Commercial Finance Corporation was the state investment bank of the day, dedicated to providing long-term capital for small and medium enterprises. The 1964 Ministry of Technology was intended by Harold Wilson to "guide and stimulate a major national effort to bring advanced technology and new processes into industry". The Industrial Reorganization Corporation was created in 1966 to promote mergers in industries that needed 'rationalisation'. During this period, Britain saw consolidation in the industries that produced, among other things, its cars, ships, machine tools, aircraft and textiles.

Perhaps unsurprisingly given the amount spent on it, the post-war industrial policy has had some successes. The temporary nationalisation of Rolls Royce and British Aerospace in the 1970s saved what were to go on to become highly profitable companies. The Isle of Dogs Enterprise Zone led to the construction of Canary Wharf.

Outside Britain, some, such as economist Ha-Joon Chang, argue that industrial policy and protection were the key to the rapid development of the infant American economy or today's Asian tigers. Even if we accept that these countries were perhaps not as free-market as is commonly suggested, there is an enormous difference between catch-up growth, seeking merely to copy existing methods with cheaper labour, and genuine innovation at the edge of our knowledge.

Even harder than trying to pick winners is trying to push back economic gravity. While politicians saw some 'success' in constraining the expansion of cities such as London and Birmingham, it turns out that this did not 'redistribute' economic activity to deprived areas such as Scotland, Wales or the North. Despite the best attempts of governments, Britain lost its traditional industries of textiles, steel and shipbuilding.

In the short term, merging rivals into giant monopolies may seem to increase economies of scale. In the long term, however, it reduces the competition and incentives that keep companies dynamically efficient. Studies of the national champions have found that none of them actually resulted in increased exports or spending on research. British Leyland found itself with the nickname of British Eland, or 'misery', in Germany.

By contrast, the end of the corporatist 'national champions' such as British Leyland and British Steel increased productivity by more than 20% and was the largest single factor in finally narrowing the productivity gap between the UK and Germany. Equally important is letting companies fail. It is estimated that the replacement of old inefficient firms with new entrants accounts for around 20–40% of all improvements in productivity.

That said, despite the inadvertent attempts of politicians to kill them off, it is simply not true that Britain no longer 'makes things'. We have developed significant specialities in pharmaceuticals, industrial chemistry, aerospace and telecoms. We are the country of Formula One as much as finance. Britain is expected to build 1.5 million cars in 2014 and could be Europe's second largest producer by 2017.[7] Around 80% of the cars we build are exported,[8] helping the UK enjoy its first trade surplus in cars in thirty-six years in 2012.[9]

While it would be complacent to say we have nothing to learn from continental countries such as France or Germany, equally we shouldn't hold them up as a perfect model to follow. Not every country can specialise in the same thing. One reason for France's higher productivity numbers is that its higher taxes encourage people to work less, while restrictive labour laws keep the least productive workers unemployed. While reducing quantity may up the average, increasing unemployment is not a price worth paying to get there.

What is more, we should be careful of the lessons we take. One reason why German cars have been so successful is not the inherent superiority of 'German engineering', but because they did not endure the paralysing trade union activities suffered by the UK and the US. In America, companies such as General Motors found themselves burdened with such high wages and pension costs that they were forced to scrimp on quality elsewhere. Only after going literally bankrupt were they able to negotiate a more sustainable deal.

More to the point, the line between manufacturing and services is already blurring. British companies design many of the world's innovative products, from the Dyson vacuum cleaner to the Raspberry Pi $25 computer. Does it really make so much a difference that the ARM microchips, designed in Cambridge and now powering the majority of the world's computers, are built in the Far East? Apple does not build its phones in California, and yet still harvests the majority of the profit. Even if a company's products are built by robots in the West rather than low-paid workers in the East, this will not bring back the kind of lifelong, well-paid, middle-skill job that many feel manufacturing used to provide. Those kinds of jobs are much more likely to be found in the service sector, where human connection is paramount, than in easily automated manufacturing.

While it is easy to create a statistic splitting our economy into a binary – manufacturing and services – a modern knowledge economy is more of a spectrum. There is not that much difference between a high-end engineering company running increasingly sophisticated models to test its new design, and a new software start-up looking to create Britain's Facebook. That start-up, in turn, has much in common with marketing, and marketing with Britain's other creative industries. They all involve highly skilled, creative employees, and invest more in research and training than in bricks and mortar.

Indeed, when you add in the costs of these 'intangible' investments, the supposed long-standing problem of British underinvestment largely disappears from the data. According to economist Jonathan Haskel, when these are included, British companies actually invest rather more than German companies.[10] Indeed, it may be the difficulty in measuring this intangible investment that explains some of the puzzling fall in the productivity numbers over the last few years.[11]

It is unlikely, however, to explain all of it. Nor should the potentially bright future for Britain as an ideas economy blind us to the difficulties it faces today.

Nobody quite understands why British productivity has fallen so much in recent years. Some point to a broken financial system, slowing the economy's natural tendency to reallocate capital from old, inefficient firms to new ones. Others argue that the data is wrong or overstated, and that the low growth numbers come from companies 'hoarding' labour due to low demand. Still others argue that our economy's efficiency was never quite as high as we let ourselves believe, and that we mistook a debt bubble for real progress.

Probably all of these explanations are true, to some extent. In some ways, it does not matter which is right. Given that we remain around 20% less efficient than America, there is clearly plenty of room for improvement. Some, such as economist Tyler Cowen, have worried that American growth has temporarily slowed as the world's most dynamic country runs out of 'low-hanging fruit'. Fortunately, that is not a problem we have to worry about yet – we may not be able to enjoy a developing country's rapid rate of growth, but we certainly should be able to close the gap with the world's leader.

The standard establishment recommendations for improving productivity are well summarised by the conclusions of the 2013 LSE Growth Commission. It recommended that Britain should focus on improving the quality of its education ("human capital"), infrastructure and provision of finance.

No doubt these three are all worthy objectives. It is hard not to notice, though, that none of them provides much of an answer to why Britain is still less efficient than America. If there is one country that shares Britain's reputation, deserved or otherwise, for underinvestment in infrastructure, a middling school system and casino finance, it is the US.

These answers are, then, at best incomplete. The record of the twentieth century was that top-down industrial policy in general, and restricting competition, not only didn't work, but actually reduced productivity.

What if we tried to increase competition instead?

Too Big to Fail

The fact that human flight was even possible was a surprise. In 1895, Lord Kelvin, discoverer of absolute zero and then president of the Royal Society, confidently declared that "heavier than air flying machines are impossible". Six years later, in 1901, the man who was imminently to prove Kelvin wrong told his brother Orville that he didn't think man would fly for another fifty years. Two years later, the Wright brothers were in the air.

But, while flight proved surprisingly doable, and, catalysed by war, was to make remarkable progress, finding a sustainable business model proved much harder. The end of the First World War was to lead to the creation of several new commercial airlines. By 1921, they were all bankrupt.

Nevertheless, aviation was clearly the way of the future. Governments in a hurry could not afford to wait for the market to figure it out. Once one country started to subsidise its airlines, the others felt obliged to follow suit, lest their national industry disappear. And, if you were going to subsidise aviation, it made sense to merge the airlines into one national carrier rather than suffer 'wasteful' duplication of routes. In 1924, the four largest British long-distance airlines were merged into the new Imperial Airways.

As it happened, the problem of international competition was soon to disappear. Rather than embrace a normal market, at the 1944 Chicago conference it was decided that aviation should be organised by bilateral treaty. The new International Air Transport Association (IATA) would act as a cartel for the industries. To change the price of a ticket, an airline would need the permission not just of IATA, but of both governments involved.[12]

Domestic industries were scarcely any better. In America, the Civil Aeronautics Board (CAB) was given the power to choose which routes airlines could fly, and to set the price they could charge. Seeking to eliminate duplication, it gave only one or two airlines the right to fly on any particular route.[13] Airlines could compete only on the quality of their food, cabin crew and the frequency of flights. Because they flew so much, only about 50% of the seats were full.[14] Yet, since the regulator would never let them go out of business, that scarcely mattered. Any increase in costs would be passed on in higher ticket prices, which the passengers would have little choice but to pay.

It happened that there were a couple of routes that the CAB didn't control, such as the flights between north and south California. Strangely enough, the absence of regulation didn't lead to predatory businesses exploiting consumers. Instead, vigorous competition led to prices much lower than comparable distances under the CAB.

Over the course of the 1970s, the CAB regulations were gradually loosened. Airlines were allowed to charge discount fares for the first time. The 1978 Airline Deregulation Act phased out the existence of the CAB itself.

The results have been dramatic. Deregulation is estimated to have saved American passengers $20 billion a year. In twenty years, traffic increased 150%.[15] Planes are now on average closer to three-quarters full.[16] The industry itself saw significant structural change, including the rise of the low-cost carriers and the hub-and-spoke model of using core airports as interconnections for their networks. Many historic airlines, such as Pan Am or TWA, did not survive the transition. Other countries, including Britain, rapidly followed America's lead. Without deregulation, there would have been no Virgin Atlantic, Easyjet or Ryanair.

American aviation was one of the first major industries to undergo deregulation. The crucial 1978 Act came before either Thatcher or Reagan took office. It seems a clear example of the benefits of competition: more choice, lower prices and faster innovation: this despite high barriers to entry, on the one hand, in the shape of the costs of buying aircraft and negotiating with airports and the regulators, and significant economies of scale, on the other. Nevertheless, competition worked.

And yet it was also something of a paradox. The post-liberalisation shakeup in the industry led to the number of airlines falling by more than half.[17] Does this imply that deregulation actually led to a decrease in competition?

The answer is no. Remember the experiments of economist Vernon Smith, which showed that markets often reach a theoretically optimum equilibrium with only a few companies. Often, given the economies of scale in an industry, an efficient market means only a few leading brands. What matters is not the number of firms, but how 'contestable' the market is: that is, how easy it would be for new companies to enter the markets, whether or not there are significant sunk costs and whether there is a similar technology level across firms.

Google is a good example. If you looked at its overwhelming dominance of the search engine market alone, a populist might say that the market is uncompetitive. But if Google were to stop meeting our needs it would only take one click for us all to switch to someone else.

While uncompetitive markets tend to be characterised by monopolies and a high concentration of firms within an industry, it does not follow, when we observe the dominance of a small number of firms within a market, that it must necessarily be uncompetitive.

For example, despite at least seven major supermarket chains (Tesco, Asda, Sainsbury's, Morrisons, Aldi, Lidl and Waitrose) and frequent price wars, there are still consistent complaints that the supermarket sector is not competitive enough. A thousand equally sized supermarkets might deliver lower profit margins, but without their highly developed logistics networks it would equally result in higher prices for consumers. In the US, Walmart has for decades led the way in improving the efficiency of its logistics, saving its customers a reported $200 billion a year.[18] Critics complain that smaller stores can't compete with its low prices – but this is, of course, the point.

Over time, markets do not just evolve in terms of specific companies within them; whole market structures change. Is it more efficient to outsource a business activity, or are the transaction costs so high that it is better to keep it in-house? How many car manufacturers are there room for in the market, and should they own their own salesrooms? Should consumers pay for journalism per article, per publication or in a bundle? Is it more efficient for a manufacturer to focus his profits on the original razor or on selling the blades?

As technology changes, different parts of an industry often find themselves alternatively disaggregated or consolidated.

When governments try to interfere with the existing structure of a market, they often find themselves overtaken by events. Take Microsoft in the 1990s. It clearly enjoyed a monopoly, and, what is more, one that was demonstrably slowing innovation in software. Once Microsoft's Internet Explorer had vanquished rival Netscape Navigator, it was left without updates for five years. And yet it is not clear that the antitrust case brought by the US Department of Justice really improved matters. It was Google and the iPhone, not the DOJ, that ultimately broke Microsoft's dominance. The specific issue on which the case was brought, of whether internet browsers should be bundled with a new computer, seems anachronistic. No computer, tablet or smartphone today comes without one.

How, then, can we decide whether an industry enjoys enough competition? When can government intervention lead to a consumer revolution, as in aviation, and when is the government just meddling in search of populist applause?

The most reliable rule of thumb is to look at why exactly new firms aren't entering the market. There was no technological reason why someone couldn't have taken on Microsoft in the 1990s. What we are really looking for are either artificial barriers to entry created by the government or significant market failures.

Monopolies by themselves are not necessarily harmful. Often they encourage other firms to innovate to catch up. Facebook has a very real monopoly, but breaking it up is unlikely to help anyone.

However, some kinds of monopolies do create problems. In some of our central utilities and infrastructure industries, it is next to impossible to have a fully free market. Given that they are too big to fail, and often given a legislated monopoly over a particular area, some regulation is appropriate.

What is not needed is to jump to the other extreme and nationalise any industry that requires a significant amount of public investment. We tried this in the post-war era, and it largely led to excessive costs.

Given that the regulator allowed them to pass on their costs to trapped consumers, many of the nationalised utilities were incredibly inefficient, overinvesting and proving unresponsive to their customers. Nobody wants to go back to the days of waiting weeks for BT to install a telephone line.

What we need, instead, is to create the institutions of a free market wherever possible, while maintaining basic regulation to tackle market failure.

Privatisation was a success. Despite its mixed record of popularity among the public, in terms of pure economic efficiency it unambiguously worked. A sectoral comparison of labour productivity growth shows that the UK had the highest productivity growth of the G7 countries in construction and phenomenal rates in electricity, gas and water, primarily due to liberalisation and regulatory reforms undertaken in electricity and gas. An analysis by the National Economic Research Associates for the Centre for Policy Studies in the early 1990s showed no negative impacts on safety, improved contributions to the Exchequer, higher profitability, better labour productivity and lower prices following privatisation.[19]

Nevertheless, the specifics of the new markets created by privatisation are unlikely to be perfect or fit for purpose forever. Designing the framework of a market on a blackboard is just as hard as designing a new product or company. There are difficult decisions to make about which parts of the industry to group together, and which to keep apart. It would not be surprising if some mistakes were made in the first round.

Perhaps the most controversial privatisation of all has been the railways.

Many of the complaints about the industry are overstated. After decades of stagnation under British Rail, the railways are once again growing. Clearly, the industry must be doing something right. The number of passengers has doubled since privatisation, and is expected to double again by 2030.[20] The majority of this cannot be attributed to higher road costs or the increasing focus of the economy on London. Passenger growth has been faster than in France, Germany or the Netherlands.[21] The private firms have delivered higher reliability and better punctuality.

Nevertheless, many problems in the industry remain. Britain has the most expensive rail tickets in Europe, despite subsidising the industry by £5 billion a year. Britain's railways are around 40% less efficient than similar systems in Europe.[22]

At present, the principal element of competition comes from the franchising system, in which private firms bid for monopoly control of a part of the network for a set duration. Even if they are successful, the rail franchises have very little flexibility to choose their own services. The vast majority of the network remains controlled by the government, either directly, through Department for Transport micro-managing, or indirectly, though the publicly owned Network Rail running the track.

There have been a few bright sparks of competition. Unusually, the East Coast Main Line has two open-access operators on the same line, Grand Central and First Hull Trains. Those stations with competition from the open-access operators saw more passenger journeys, lower fares and greater passenger satisfaction than those without.[23]

Equally, the rail freight industry has always acted on the directly competitive model. It has been even more transformed than passenger services, with rapid growth and increases in efficiency.[24] Unit costs have come down by 35% between 1998–1999 and 2008–2009, compared with a 10% increase on the passenger side.[25] Freight is a dynamic market, with frequent new entrants and consolidations of the old firms.

When the railways in Britain were first developed by the private sector, they did not choose the industry structure we have now imposed on them. Instead, a single company would own both trains and the track. The original privatisation system rejected this option, believing it would limit competition.

One way to test this out for sure would be to break up the current national Network Rail into new, private regional franchises. These would have the power to merge with the parallel franchises for running the trains if they thought this was more efficient, or, equally, they could keep to something closer to today's model. We should let these franchises issue their own bonds for investment, and even develop integrated housing and transport investment.

When we think of uncompetitive markets we tend to picture utilities such as transport or energy, but there are many other industries in Britain that are both too uncompetitive and implicitly protected by government. Banking, in particular, has particularly high barriers to entry, many of which are policy-induced.

Metro Bank, founded in 2010, is the first new entrant to the high street in over 100 years. Government regulation and the implicit subsidy of too-big-to-fail make it incredibly difficult for new entrants. The big four – RBS, Lloyds, Barclays and HSBC – control 78% of the current account market. Maybe, though, this is just a sign of their success in attracting customers?

This seems incredibly far-fetched in this instance. They are some of the least popular banks with customers.[26] Britain's banks receive 10,000 complaints per day. According to a recent *Which?* survey, 59% of customers would switch accounts if it were easier to do so.[27] Poor service is compounded by deficient IT systems, illustrated by the computer breakdown at RBS in 2012 that blocked account access for millions of customers. Currently, just 2% of bank depositors switch banks each year.[28]

In 2011, the banking sector committed to guaranteeing that accounts would be switched on request within seven working days by September 2013. However, it still remains unduly cumbersome to switch accounts, undermining the greatest leverage the consumer has. According to *Which?*, three-quarters of customers believe that the introduction of portable bank account numbers would make switching banks easier. The answer is to give customers a portable banking code, and require the banks to adopt a common IT system (also accessible to new entrants). The technology exists, although it would require a significant transition period and would require substantial costs to establish.

To achieve this, banks would need to establish a clearing system in common. Such a clearing system could hold all bank accounts, with an identifying code to establish which bank holds the account. This would have enormous advantages for competition and consumer choice.

Customer switching would be almost instantaneous, causing the banks to compete to retain customers and gain new ones. Customers could transfer their accounts but keep their existing account number if they wish. Any newly authorised bank would be able to buy a licence to use the system, removing the advantage of the long-established clearers. In the event of a future financial collapse, accounts could be easily transferred from failed institutions to sound ones, reducing the risk of a 'run' on the banks.

A number of discrete policy measures would further help newcomers. First, licensing of new banks by the Financial Services

Authority (FSA) is unduly cumbersome, because opaque and moving deadlines create unnecessary uncertainty, which deters investors. On average, new financial firms are waiting a record 21.6 weeks for a decision on approval.[29] Second, FSA scrutiny of applicant business plans has an in-built preference for a strong high street presence, which goes against the commercial grain (with many banks reducing the number of costly outlets) and imposes high costs on start-ups looking to draw on online or telephone banking to innovate more competitive products and rates for customers. Third, the FSA takes a conservative approach to personnel, favouring the appointment of existing banking executives.[30] While experience is important, this approach risks entrenching an 'old boys' network and discourages new thinking. Fourth, the capital requirements expected of new banks are unduly high – based on the forecast balance sheet in five years' time – which discourages new entrants. Fifth, liquidity requirements – with specific regard to quickly acquired deposits, larger deposits and online account deposits – have the effect of deterring many new banks. Sixth, the lack of a common clearing system accessible to new entrants penalises prospective new banks.

Privately, many with experience of applying for FSA licensing are scathing about the process, claiming there is an unwarranted cultural bias that invariably concludes that too many banks are just 'too small to start'. Applicants are reticent about speaking publicly, for fear of entirely falling out of favour with FSA officials. Equally, the one new bank to successfully enter the marketplace – Metro Bank – reported that, due to the regulatory hurdles, it only expected to break even in its fourth year of trading.[31]

While many are aware of the competitive problems in rail and banking, an equally worrying sector is journalism – and the overriding reason is the BBC.

Few would approve of the government subsidising its own newspaper, even if it were officially held at arm's length. Instead of looking to a single authoritative voice, we trust in the vicious competition of a raucous free press to hold the government to account. As much as an official broadcaster might try to be 'neutral', the better way of getting at the truth is often to hear both sides of the argument. While an unconstrained press might have its ugly side, it is surely better to err on the side of too much press freedom than too little.

When the BBC was founded, on first the radio and subsequently television, the lack of spectrum made this competitive solution impossible. Instead, it was decided to create a national broadcaster.

At the beginning of its existence, the BBC did at least worry about making sure that it did not undermine the other media. The original BBC service was not broadcast until after 7 pm so as not to compete with newspapers, until the fast-moving events of the General Strike made this untenable.[32]

Today, the corporation has no such compunction. It already accounts for around 70% of television news, by far the most important source today – and its share has been growing. It is barely less dominant on the internet, where it enjoys a 40% share.[33] It is by far the largest provider of radio, providing around half of all hours listened to.[34]

It is hardly a new insight that newspapers are struggling, as readership of traditional paper-based publications falls and classified advertising moves to the internet. The industry is in the middle of a difficult transition to digital. Many different business models are being experimented with, from paywalls to voluntary subscriptions. What is clear is that the worlds of audio, video and text are increasingly blurring.

The last thing the industry needs is a publicly subsidised rival, undercutting it in a way that is impossible to compete with. This is bad enough on the national level, but even worse for local journalism. The music industry was nearly killed by the presence of a free rival in piracy. In news, the free rival is not only not illegal; it is mandatory.

In an age of HBO, Sky Arts, YouTube and Khan Academy, we hardly need the BBC as a guarantee of quality entertainment or education. The technological reasons for a single licence fee or national broadcaster have long faded as we have entered an age of effectively limitless spectrum. The only real distinction between the BBC and Sky is that the latter doesn't try to send you to jail if you don't want to pay its subscription fee.

That said, it would be churlish not to point out that the BBC is popular for good reasons. It has a world-class reputation, and is genuinely a focus of national affection. Our goal should be to secure the corporation's future for the long term, on a sustainable basis, while preventing it from turning the British media into an unhealthy monoculture. The easiest way to do this would be to reform the licence fee. By making the licence fee a subscription service, such that access to BBC channels would be turned off in the result of non-payment, we would solve most of the problems with the institution. Indeed, the proposed decriminalisation of the licence fee seems a first step along this route.

In an increasingly globalised and digital media market, the licence fee is clearly an anachronism. The laws sustaining it have already fallen behind the technological reality of how many people watch TV. You do not need to pay the licence fee if you are just watching the iPlayer on your iPad.

While the rivalry of competition is important, what increases productivity most drastically of all is a complete paradigm shift. Microsoft's monopoly was not toppled by a clone of itself, but by a simple search engine. Low-cost airlines like Southwest Airline and Easyjet completely changed the assumptions upon which the legacy carriers had built their business model.

What happens when we get a revolution?

Regulation and Revolution

If the world's economy has gone through two big shifts so far – from agriculture to industry and then from industry to services – some believe that we are now standing on the verge of a third.

As recently as 1998, it was possible for economist Paul Krugman to argue that "the internet's impact on the economy [will be] no greater than the fax machine's".[35] Nobody believes that anymore. Already, the internet has massively disrupted retail, telecoms, photography, music, film, television, publishing, journalism and tourism. Away from the economic sphere, it has spurred democratic revolutions, changed the way we date, and radically shifted our notion of privacy. In the next few years it seems to be on the verge of revolutionising taxi services through Uber, the way we exchange money through Bitcoin or Square, or the way we learn through Khan Academy or Udacity. Software, in Marc Andreessen's phrase, is eating the world.

If the importance of software is not going away, hardware is just getting started. The combination of powerful AI, persistent networks and commoditised components is creating a new revolution. If you ignore computers, the average way of living today is not so different from that of a family in the 1950s: we drive a car to an office, shop or factory; relax at home in front of the television. Without giving in too far to technological utopianism, it is not impossible that this will all change in the next fifty years. A robot will do the work in the factory, a drone will deliver your shopping while you work from home, and when you do need to get somewhere your car will drive itself.

Even in more mundane ways, technology could radically change the shape of many of today's industries. Take banking. There is no real technological reason why sending money to a foreign country should be any harder than sending an email. New technologies for securely storing and transferring money, such as Paypal and Bitcoin, are still in their early days, but it seems likely that something like them will eventually offer a cheaper option. Companies like Square are helping small retailers to avoid today's high payment-processing fees, while the idea of crowdfunding is slowly spreading from arts projects to small businesses.

The British economy has always been a leading indicator of trends in the world economy. Fortunately, we remain in a good position to benefit from this coming technological wave. In his book *Average Is Over*, Tyler Cowen argues that the people who will benefit most from automation are those with the right scarce skills in "STEM fields, finance, management and marketing".[36] This is about as good a description of Britain's economic specialities as you can get. As the home to both Alan Turing and Saatchi & Saatchi, we should do just fine.

The biggest danger to this innovation will come from excessive regulation.

While it is important to protect customers, it is also important not to forget the opportunity cost that delaying new innovation creates. Given that 90% of traffic accidents come from driver error, the arrival of self-driving cars could save 1,500 lives a year in Britain, and a million a year worldwide. More modestly, it does not really make sense for every Western nation to have a separate bureaucracy testing new drugs. This delays their introduction, even when they have been approved elsewhere, and is costing hundreds of lives.[37] Ten years after they were approved and went into wide use in France, Americans are still not allowed to use sunscreens that block a wider range of cancer-causing UV rays.[38]

By its nature, regulation is backwards-looking and guided by excessive fear of the worst-case scenario. We often forget how worrying new innovations such as the telephone or camera appeared to the general public when they first emerged. Back in the nineteenth century, the arrival of the steam train saw some arguing that parliament should restrict its speed to eight or nine miles an hour.

We are not so much more enlightened. Venture capitalist Peter Thiel argues that it is no coincidence that we have seen most technological progress in the digital technologies, such as computing, which are least regulated. Although it was difficult to point to who exactly they were harming, excessive regulation stopped health start-up 23andMe offering a $99 genetic analysis kit,[39] or InTrade a wide range of prediction markets. All too often, regulation has been exploited by threatened incumbents seeking to shut down new rivals. Taxi drivers have tried to ban Uber, while car salesmen try to prevent Tesla from selling its cars directly to its customers.

To have regulation hold back innovation, of course, you need some innovation in the first place. Two things stand out about the above examples.

The first is that they overwhelmingly come from new, small companies. This is not always true – drugs are still largely created by pharmaceutical giants, while today's tech firms, such as Google, are showing an admirable unwillingness to stop taking risks – but start-ups still punch above their weight in radical, disruptive innovation.

But, just as strikingly, the majority of the dynamic new companies we hear about today are, of course, American. Given the first-mover advantages of being the pioneer in a new industry, it is no surprise that many of these start-ups go on to be the successful corporations of tomorrow.

Why is the US so good at starting new companies?

There are many reasons, from culture to education. But one that shouldn't be underestimated is the ease with which you can take a risk by creating a company.

Despite the caricature of America as a harsh frontier society where you either sink or swim, the US actually has one of the most liberal systems of bankruptcy in the world. While this may cause some problems when the system is abused and zombie companies get tied up in bureaucracy, it also means that entrepreneurs are not overly penalised when their first business doesn't go as well as they had hoped. It is an important element of the far more forgiving culture towards failure that powers their entrepreneurship.

Starting any new business is incredibly risky. According to the ONS, around half of new businesses fail in the first five years.[40] While we probably shouldn't copy the US system wholesale, in Britain at present administration only applies to limited companies and partnerships, leaving tens of thousands of small businesses without any protection at all.

What if the company is a success, however?

After building a sustainable business model, perhaps the hardest step in building a new company is taking on staff.

America does not have the world's best infrastructure, the most educated students or a financial system thought of as more concerned with 'Main Street than Wall Street'. These days even its taxes are not particularly low compared with some of its competitors.

What it does have, according to the Heritage Foundation Index of Economic Freedom, is the most liberal system of labour regulation in the world.[41] It scores 97.1 out of 100 on their index. By contrast, the UK scores just 73.1, putting us in fifty-third position in 2014. This score has been getting worse – nine years ago, we scored 79 and were twentieth.[42]

Excessive labour regulation acts as the ultimate barrier to entry. Entrenched businesses can afford the burden, whether through a large HR department or by passing on the costs to their customers. For start-ups, by contrast, it can suck up the time and attention that should be spent on finding their business model.

Over the last three decades, the burden of employment regulation has swollen six times in size.[43] This comes with a price tag attached. In 2011, British business spent £112 billion to comply with the administrative requirements – the equivalent of 7.9% of GDP, or the entire output of a country the size of Singapore.[44] It is estimated that the impact of the presumption of a 48-hour week under the Working Time Directive costs the UK economy more than £3.6 billion every year.[45]

Our ambition should be to make Britain the easiest country in the world to start and grow a new company. While our membership of the European Union constrains some of what we can do, we should do whatever we can to cut the burden of employment regulation. We could even take inspiration from Germany itself. In 2004, businesses with fewer than ten employees in Germany were made exempt from the need to provide a cause when dismissing an employee. Why not allow the first ten employees of a new company to be treated as self-employed for a set number of years, so as to be exempted from a raft of employment legislation and tax law? This would allow new companies, which are not established, not to have to deal with the burden of calculating and collecting PAYE, for example. The problem at the moment is that labour market regulations are disproportionately damaging to challenger businesses, which face considerable uncertainty over both the likelihood of their businesses' success and the staffing implications. Flexibility, then, could have substantial benefits.

Instead of trying to pick winners or rationalise industries, we need to allow room for small start-ups to experiment. Yet politicians often delude themselves that they can identify the industries of the future. History suggests otherwise. We need a flexible, competitive economy unburdened by unnecessary regulation in order to allow the truly best industries and companies to emerge. What policy can achieve is to set the framework for these competitive markets to operate, provided the government takes into account the effects regulations imposed by itself will have on competition. At the moment there are many important established markets where the forces of competition are desperately needed.

THE FREE ENTERPRISE MANIFESTO – INDUSTRIAL POLICY:

1) We should introduce a range of measures to increase competition across UK industries:
   a. Full account portability in the banking system.
   b. Separating Network Rail into regional franchises.
   c. Converting the BBC licence fee into a voluntary subscription.
2) We should reform bankruptcy law to give individual entrepreneurs more protection.
3) We should allow the first ten employees to be registered as self-employed.

5 The Market for Energy

Our current energy policy rests on an expensive bet that oil prices will rise, while the cost of renewables comes down. Unfortunately, crucial uncertainties remain over the path of oil prices, the political realities in emerging nations, the climate and the future cost of renewables. Given this uncertainty, markets remain the best way to increase energy supply and manage climate change. Rather than try to plan future technologies, the government would do better to restrict itself to subsidies and prizes for advances in basic research.

An Inconvenient Truth

In the middle of the last decade, fossil fuel prices seemed to be on an ever-upwards path. Peak oil was imminent. While the oil fields were draining away, the level of carbon in the atmosphere was growing. In Britain, Tony Blair became convinced that climate change was the most important problem the world faced, and set himself the urgent task of converting the rest of the world to his view. 2006 was the year of both Al Gore's *An Inconvenient Truth* and   David Cameron's visit to the Arctic Circle.

The UK, it was decided, would set an example for the rest of the world. The government commissioned the Stern Review, which was to become famous for its claim that it would cost 1% of world GDP to prevent damage of up to 20%. We would give up our addiction to fossil fuels, replacing our power stations with new zero-carbon sources of energy. In the short term, this might require substantial subsidy, but in the long term it would actually prove cheaper than remaining dependent on fossil fuel reserves. Those forms of transport that could not realistically be converted to run on electricity, such as aviation, would have to be strictly limited. There could be no possibility of a third runway at Heathrow.

In nine short years, however, almost every assumption behind this strategy has been challenged. The arrival of the financial crisis reminded everyone of the importance of cheap energy and connectivity for growth. Oil production began to grow again, while oil demand now seems as likely to fall as to rise. The commercial deployment of shale gas in the US exceeded all expectations. In the second half of 2014, oil prices halved. Thanks to the development of new technologies to harness unconventional resources, the world seems to be facing an age of abundant hydrocarbons. The estimated costs from aggressive carbon reduction seem to be growing, while cheaper adaptation looks ever more attractive.

The traditional objectives of energy policy are to ensure a cheap, green and ample supply. Instead, households complain bitterly of ever higher bills, climate activists are in despair, and Britain is rapidly shutting down its power stations without replacements lined up to take their place. Between 2010 and 2013, the average prices of gas and electricity paid for by UK households in real terms rose by 18% and 9%, respectively.[1] In 2013, Ofgem had to warn of a 1 in 4 chance of blackouts.[2] International climate change negotiations have largely collapsed, while costly UK and European initiatives to cut emissions seem to be having zero effect on world emissions.

Our current approach to energy and climate change policy does not seem to be pleasing anyone. What's gone wrong?

Global Warming

The maths seemed very clear. All else being   equal, basic physics suggested that a doubling of the carbon density   from pre-industrial levels would create worldwide warming of 1.1°C. Unfortunately, all else is not equal, and there are many other feedback effects in the atmosphere, such as water vapour, cloud formation or the melting of ice. The consensus is that overall sensitivity to a doubling is likely to be between 1.5 and 4.5°C.[3] As a rough rule of thumb, warming up to 2°C could actually be a net positive to the planet, between 2°C and 3°C would likely cause harm, and anything significantly above this could be catastrophic.

Accordingly, the international community has set itself a target of limiting overall warming to 2°C. This, in turn, implies that the atmospheric concentration of carbon needs to be limited to around 550 ppm, around double the pre-industrial levels of 275 ppm. According to the UK's Committee on Climate Change, this implies that global emissions need to halve by 2050. Allowing for the fact that world population is expected to grow, UK emissions need to be reduced by 80% by 2050 compared with 1990 levels.[4]

Energy generation produces around 40% of the UK's carbon emissions. The second largest source of emissions, transport, is technologically harder to decarbonise in the short term and, in any case, will eventually require its own zero-carbon electricity supply. Successive governments have therefore chosen to focus most of their climate change strategy on decarbonising energy.[5]

Ultimately, climate change is a global problem, and accordingly any policy response needs to be co-ordinated at a global level. In 1988, the United Nations created the Intergovernmental Panel on Climate Change (IPCC) in order to synthesise and summarise the best evidence on climate change and its impact.

The IPCC's first report served as the basis for the UN Framework Convention on Climate Change, signed in 1992 in Rio de Janeiro. Over 172 countries and 116 heads of state or governments came together to discuss a unified strategy. The eventual agreement committed its signatories to "stabilize greenhouse gas concentrations in the atmosphere at a level that would prevent dangerous anthropogenic interference with the climate system". This was formalised into the Kyoto Protocol in 1997, setting binding emission targets for developed countries from 2005 – although the US infamously refused to ratify the protocol, and Canada withdrew in 2011.

By the 2011 Durban UN Climate Change Conference, it was clear that the negotiations had broken down. Of the major players, only the EU was interested in creating a second Kyoto with binding emissions caps. None of the US, China, India, Japan, Canada or Russia would sign up. The best the conference could agree to was to come to an agreement by 2015, which in turn would only come into effect by 2020.

At present, there is little sign that growth in world emissions is slowing, let alone reversing. Whom you blame for this depends on how you slice the data. From the territorial or production point of view – allocating emissions by the country in which they are actually produced – moderate reductions in the first world are being massively outweighed by growth in emerging markets. Between them, China and India are expected to open the equivalent of three new coal power stations a week. Europe would need to build an extra 1,000 wind turbines a week to compensate for this.[6]

An arguably more useful point of view allocates emissions according to whom they are being generated for. Much of China's growing emissions are being used to generate cheap consumer goods for the West. If you try to allocate emissions on this basis, Britain's 20% reduction between 1990 and 2009 turns into a 20% increase.[7] In recent years, emissions have radically dropped, but this seems almost certain to be just an effect of the recession.

But perhaps this is too short-sighted a view. The EU may not be able to force the rest of the world to cut its emissions, the argument goes, but perhaps it could serve as a model of what a post-carbon economy could look like. If it could develop renewable technologies fast enough, it could drop their price sufficiently that other nations would give up their fossil fuels voluntarily. This couldn't just be confined to a lab, as true innovation would only happen through learning by doing. The EU would have to turn itself into one large experiment, turning off its old power supplies immediately and switching to the new renewables.

Indeed, there was good news. Government predictions showed that the price of fossil fuels was only going to go up. In the long term, if the government could find and pick the right renewables technologies, they could actually save Europeans money. Investing hundreds of billions of pounds in renewable technologies might be a bet, but what was the worst that could happen?

The Bet

The president's warning was serious. The energy crisis that had consumed much of the last decade was not going away. Unless profound changes were made, the next decade would see the world "demanding more oil than it can produce...Each new inventory of world oil reserves has been more disturbing than the last. World oil production can probably keep going up for another six or eight years. But...it can't go up much more. Demand will overtake production."[8]

Jimmy Carter was not the first person to warn of peak oil, and he would not be the last. In the years following his 1977 speech, the high level of prices encouraged development of new oil fields outside OPEC's control. Crude oil prices never returned to the low level of the 1960s, but nor did they keep climbing. For twenty years they were largely static.

The concept of 'peak oil' originated with geologist M. King Hubbert. In 1956, Hubbert predicted that American domestic production would peak over the next fifteen years. Supporters of the theory went on to extrapolate the model to the world as a whole.

For some, peak oil meant not higher petrol prices, but an existential threat to civilisation. Oil was so central to the workings of the modern world, under this theory, that civilisation would not be able to cope with its loss.

This was always, to put it mildly, unlikely. In the worst case, there was never a realistic scenario in which oil production declined faster than our ability to build replacement nuclear power. The Fisher–Tropsch process allows coal to be converted into oil, and becomes commercially viable when there is roughly a four to one ratio between the prices of oil and coal. South Africa already generates significant proportions of its oil in this way.

A more modest peak oil hypothesis argued simply that we will run out of oil at some point in the next few decades. Just as American oil production declined, so will the world's.

There is, however, a significant difference between local and global markets. The rate of oil production always depends on both the world price and the cost of extraction. In the local context, it makes sense to focus first on oil fields that are easiest to harvest. If you run out of easy options, it is cheapest to import the oil from somewhere else. In the world as a whole, that is not an option. Once the world price starts to increase, there is an incentive everywhere to develop more marginal fields and test new technologies.

Presently, much of the Earth's crust remains unexplored, while recovery rates keep increasing. According to BP's data, proven total world oil reserves continue to maintain a steady upwards trend. New reserves are continually being discovered, as, for example, in Brazil, Canada or Norway, or off the coast of Brazil or the Falkland Islands.[9] While total world oil production dipped at the height of the recession, it has since returned to the steady upwards trend it has followed since the mid-1980s.

Leonardo Maugeri of the Harvard Kennedy Center argues that we now know of around 16 trillion barrels of recoverable oil, compared with a 2010 world consumption of 32.3 billion barrels. He argues that the only countries that are likely to see their production capacity reduced between 2011 and 2020 are Mexico, Norway, Iran and the

UK. In any case, it is very difficult to see us running out of oil within the next thirty or so years, or the life of an average power plant.[10]

The most modest peak oil hypothesis of all simply argues that oil prices will continue to climb as demand increases faster than supply. We may never strictly run out, but each new barrel will become harder for us to get access to.

But, in recent years, confidence in even this limited conclusion has been shaken.

While conventional fossil fuels are found in concentrated reservoirs, so-called unconventional reserves are far more distributed throughout the rock. This makes them far harder to siphon off through drilling. To access them affordably requires the bringing together of several technologies: better seismic exploration technologies to locate the reserves, 'fracking' to split apart the rock, and horizontal drilling to retrieve the fuel.

These technologies were first brought together and perfected by an American entrepreneur, George Mitchell, in the middle of the last decade. As a result, shale gas rapidly took over the American market, growing from 1.6% of the US natural gas market in 2000 to 23.1% by 2010.[11] It is now predicted to rise to 50% by 2035.[12] Indeed, it was so successful that it has led to a collapse in US gas prices. From being the world's largest gas importer, the US is now largely self-sufficient.

While the development of shale gas has proved controversial, most of the safety complaints seem overblown. The Royal Society and the Royal Academy of Engineering both agree that the technology is safe.[13] There have been no verified cases or reasons to believe in the risk of groundwater contamination; shale gas production does not cause taps to burn; the use of water resources is not noticeably greater than other industrial processes; the impact on landscape is relatively limited compared with other forms of energy; the 'earthquakes' caused by fracking are extremely minor.[14] While it is not a renewable source of fuel, it produces around 50% of the carbon emissions of coal. Since the middle of the decade, US CO_2 emissions have rapidly fallen.[15]

In Britain, there remains significant uncertainty about the level of technically recoverable shale gas. It is, however, likely to be large. In 2010, the British Geological Survey estimated that the UK might have 150 billion cubic metres (bcm) of recoverable gas. However, by 2013 the BGS was estimating that the Bowland Shale layer could potentially provide recoverable resources of 1,800 to 13,000 bcm. To put this in context, the UK currently has around 1,466 bcm in conventional gas reserves, and annual consumption is 77 bcm.[16] A recent Institute of Directors report argued that shale gas could be "a new North Sea for Britain", create tens of thousands of jobs, reduce the need for imports and generate significant tax revenues.[17]

One reason shale has developed so much more rapidly in America than in Britain is the US system of mineral rights. The 1934 Petroleum (Production) Act in Britain nationalised the ownership of oil and gas, whereas in America a landholder owns the right to minerals beneath their land. That gives them much more incentive to allow drilling, and lets them share in any bounty.

One radical option to speed up the development of shale in the UK would be to return mineral rights back to land owners. However, even without this step we could do more through the tax system to ensure that local communities benefit from development in their area.

Another important difference with the US energy market is that it is much more isolated than Britain's. Thanks to its interconnectors with the continent, the UK's energy prices are set on the world market. That means that any increase in supply will only have an indirect, diluted effect on domestic energy prices – although, of course, if shale gas is exploited across Europe the world price will come down as well. Even if shale gas didn't reduce UK prices at all, it would still bring in significant tax revenue. Oil prices are set on a world market too – but few would argue that the North Sea oil didn't benefit the country. Even Tony Benn, albeit through gritted teeth, was forced to publicly declare that the anniversary of the first oil flowing "should from then on be a day of national celebration".[18]

What is more, shale gas could just be the beginning of the hydrocarbon boom. Further technological advances have created the possibility of increasing the recovery rate on existing fields and cost-effectively harvesting other 'unconventional' fuels such as shale oil, tar sands, coal-bed methane and tight gas. After declining for decades, US oil production is once again growing.[19] Oil is much more of a world market than gas, so, even if the UK doesn't directly participate, a successful commercialisation of shale oil in America would have a huge impact on British energy markets.

Critics of shale development argue that it is a distraction from meeting our climate change targets. Even if the world now looks to enjoy ample fossil fuel reserves, we cannot burn those reserves without risking a dangerous level of climate change. Moreover, shale gas is an expensive distraction from the unofficial 2030 decarbonisation target. The Committee for Climate Change argues that it makes little sense to ramp up gas in the short term, when within twenty years we largely need to transition away from fossil fuels altogether.

It is more than possible, of course, that the hype over unconventional technologies will prove overblown. They may never prove as cheap to access as conventional supplies. Nobody really knows what lies buried under the UK's soil, and our supplies of shale gas could prove disappointing. Perhaps resistant local communities and overzealous regulation will stop the industry from ever getting off the ground. Oil prices could stop their current fall and start climbing again.

But the government's bet looks a lot less sure than it once did. After all, supply is still growing faster than demand. Over the last ten years, proved reserves have been growing by about 2.5% a year, while demand growth is less than 1%. The rate of demand growth seems unlikely to more than double. Indeed, many analysts have now swung in completely the opposite direction, and are predicting 'peak oil demand' due to increased fuel efficiency and substitution for gas.[20]

But if the old technologies are showing a new life and cheaper costs, what of the renewables?

Too Cheap to Meter

In 1954, Lewis Strauss, the then chairman of the United States Atomic Energy Commission, predicted a bright future. The next generation, he thought, could look forward to the end of famine across the world, a slowing down of the ageing process and, most famously of all, "electrical energy too cheap to meter". Two years later, the same prediction was repeated by one of the twentieth century's brightest minds, mathematician and economist John Von Neumann.

Imagine if this really had come to pass. We would no longer have to worry about climate change, fuel poverty or blackmail from foreign dictators. Unlimited energy would make potential solutions to other significant problems affordable, from desalination plants to tackle water shortages to increasing food production.

Given this potential utopia, it is little surprise that we have poured so many resources into subsidising research into new sources of energy.

At present, the UK uses on average around 40 GW of power, the equivalent of 16,000,000 kettles being used at the same time.[21] At peak times, energy use is around 40% more than this, or about 55 GW. A reasonable mid-estimate for our power generation needs in 2050 would be three times today's average, or 120 GW.

Is it ever possible to generate this through renewables?

At the moment, we are projected to spend around £100 billion over the next decade on wind power. Onshore wind generates around $2W/m^2$, implying that to meet electricity demand you'd need to cover 25% of the country.[22] You would need to cover the entirety of the UK's shallow water (less than 25 m) with wind turbines to produce 120 GW.[23] Obviously, the deeper you are prepared to go, the more electricity you are able to generate, but the engineering considerations and cost become still more challenging. By its very nature, offshore wind seems unlikely ever to be truly cost-competitive with gas.

Future generations of solar power technology seem to have a better chance of becoming cost-competitive. For over thirty years now, the final cost of solar power has decreased by around 7% a year.[24] There seems to be no fundamental technological reason for this Moore's Law-like regularity – unlike silicon chips, you cannot reliably increase performance of solar panels simply by miniaturisation – and so this cost reduction could easily bottom out, as many forecasts predict.[25]

Nevertheless, if this trend were to continue for the next decade, solar power would achieve grid parity in a significant proportion of the world. Current technology is around 10–20% efficient at converting solar power into electricity. While we are unlikely to achieve the theoretical maximum of 60%, technologies exist in the lab at up to 40% efficiency.

Unfortunately, in the short term Britain is unlikely to benefit much from solar power. Given our climate and latitude, and an average efficiency of 10%, solar panels can only generate around $10 W/m^2$. This implies that to meet current UK demand you'd need to cover around 5% of the UK's land area in solar panels.[26] While this may not sound that much, it is more than triple the current proportion of the UK that is built on – around 1.5%.[27]

Another possibility would be to import solar power from the much hotter, more consistent and less densely populated desert areas. This would still be a considerable undertaking, however. One calculation suggests that to meet Europe and North Africa's electricity consumption you'd need to build a square of panels around 600 km by 600 km across in the Sahara Desert.[28]

In short, while it is technically feasible for renewable sources to provide the UK's energy in the future, offshore wind power seems unlikely to become cost-competitive, while solar power will require either continual progress or complex geopolitical arrangements. Moreover, renewables will only make a real difference if we at the same time solve the problem of cheap battery storage. Today, the intermittency of renewables means they often have to be backed up by fossil fuel or nuclear power supplies, undercutting any cost or environmental advantage.

While solar power may eventually become cost-competitive, this is unlikely to be the case for the UK until at least the mid-2020s – long after British energy companies have had to lock in their investments to meet the government's targets.

In 2009, the EU committed itself to the 20-20-20 targets: by 2020, a 20% cut in greenhouse gas emissions compared with 1990, raising the share of renewables to 20% of the energy supply, and a 20% cut in energy consumption from improvements in efficiency. Because the UK started from a very low level, it was given a lower target of 15% by 2020. (For the most part, there seems no reasoning beyond aesthetics for choosing 20%.) The EU is now pushing for a 40% binding cut in greenhouse emissions target for 2030 compared with 1990, a legally binding target of 27% renewables in the final energy balance of the EU by the same time, and a similar target for energy consumption from improved efficiency.

Given that the main objective seems to be decarbonisation, it is unclear what the rationale is of requiring a share of the energy supply beyond that to be in renewables. 'Green industrial policy' is unlikely to prove more accurate at picking winners than the traditional kind. The lesson we learned from failed support in the past was that markets don't need government support to scale up when products are ready to go. Governments are far more likely to have a positive impact if they restrict themselves to subsidising basic research and development, rather than trying to plan the course of the industry.

Even better than straight subsidies, however, would be spending the money on a new generation of prizes. These could be designed in collaboration with scientists and industry, pinpointing specific problems, such as battery technology or simply driving down costs.

Instead of guaranteeing a high price for wind power, why not just offer a generous reward for the first person to achieve true grid parity?

By this point, prizes have a long history of use. The British Navy's prize of 1714 discovered that it was a humble clockmaker, rather than the leading astronomers of the day, who could best solve the problem of determining longitude. The French Academy's 12,000 franc prize for the development of artificial alkali in 1775 helped catalyse the inorganic chemistry industry. The $25,000 Orteig Prize inspired Charles Lindbergh to fly across the Atlantic in 1927, while the $10 million Ansari X prize spurred on a new low-cost private sector space industry in 2004. The current government, working with NESTA, has introduced a £10 million prize fund to help tackle global antibiotic resistance.

The prizes do not have to be this romantic or dramatic to work. Prizes for relatively modest goals can work too. In 2011, the US Department of Energy's $10 million L Prize successfully encouraged the development of new ultra-efficient LED lamps.

Rather than pick winners, prizes allow the winners to come to us. As we discovered with John Harrison and his watch in 1714, solutions often come from unexpected sources. Given that most new things fail, we need to try many approaches rather than fixate on a politically favoured solution. Prizes can encourage dozens of teams to work on a problem at the same time, multiplying the impact of a single prize fund. Nor does this multiplication have to represent waste in the private sector. The experience so far from prizes such as the X Prize for space, or DARPA's prizes for self-driving cars, is that often, after the competition is over, the winning teams will merge and compete to form the seeds of a new industry.

Unfortunately, 'Green Industrial Policy' is far from the only intervention politicians have undertaken in energy.

The Market for Energy?

In 1982, the Secretary of State for Energy Nigel Lawson made a speech that was to come to be seen as, in the words of economist Dieter Helm, a "defining moment".[29] "The Market for Energy" did not just set the strategy for the next twenty years in Britain, but would, in turn, influence change across the whole of Europe. Lawson's view was simple: "I do *not* see the government's task as being to try to plan the future shape of energy production and consumption ... the main spur must be competition."

This was revolutionary. In the immediate aftermath of the Second World War, the vast majority of the UK's energy sector was nationalised. The Central Electricity Board was already under state control, and to this was added the National Coal Board in 1947, the British Energy Authority in 1948, the Gas Council in 1948 and the United Kingdom Atomic Energy Authority in 1954. Over the next thirty years, the industry was gradually rationalised into effectively a vertically integrated monopoly. Like most nationalised industries, the sector depended on the 'predict and provide' principle: energy demand grew at an average 7% a year,[30] and the state's job was to ensure that supply grew at least this fast.

The vast majority of electricity came from coal-powered generators, with gas dedicated to domestic heating. Nuclear power was seen as the power of the future, especially in the aftermath of the Suez Crisis. While Britain was never to embrace nuclear power as wholeheartedly as France, by 1990 around 20% of the country's electricity came from nuclear (compared with 80% from coal).

By the 1970s, the problems with the nationalised industries were becoming clear. Nuclear power had failed to become cost-effective compared with coal. The OPEC oil crisis implied that investing in nuclear power might still be worthwhile, but there was significant uncertainty about the best choice of technology. Governments were forced to try to bully oil companies in a desperate attempt to secure supply. Coal, meanwhile, was dogged by repeated industrial action. Britain found itself suffering from power outages, and was even forced at one point to adopt a three-day working week.

Trying to buy off the striking miners, governments in both parties committed to a 'Plan for Coal', reversing the long-term decline in the sector's output and unemployment, and relying on the fuel as Britain's primary fuel source up till the millennium.

More fundamentally, it became clear that there was little incentive in the industry to cut costs or act in the best interests of consumers. This was bad enough in the fairly stable post-war years, but would become disastrous in the 1980s as many of the assumptions on which the government's strategy were built proved false: the decline in industry after the 1980s recession meant that the optimistic predictions of demand from the Plan for Coal proved way too high; world fossil fuel prices did not keep rising, but fell; gas was not a premium, scarce fuel that had to be reserved for domestic use. Britain soon found itself with an excess supply of coal.

While Lawson's vision of a competitive energy market may have been simple enough, implementing it was to take over twenty years. First, British Gas was sold off as a regulated monopoly in 1985, then the government's final stake in BP by 1987. The 1989 Electricity Act split the electricity industry into three separate markets: power generation (the new National Power and PowerGen); transmission (the National Grid); and distribution (twelve new Regional Electricity Companies (RECs)). The price for electricity was to be set in a unified pool, ensuring adequate supply. Over the course of the 1990s, this structure would be further refined as British Gas was broken up, competition was gradually extended, allowing industrial and finally domestic consumers to contract out of the pool, and the RECs gradually consolidated. Finally, in 2003, price controls for the majority of the industry were ended.

The most dramatic impact of the newly privatised industry was the first 'dash for gas'. As it became obvious that abundant supplies of natural gas existed, European restrictions on using it as a power supply were lifted. This proved enough to kill off most of Britain's nuclear ambitions.

The liberalising reforms arguably neared their high-water mark in 1998, when all domestic energy consumers were able to switch supplier for the first time and wholesale markets were liberalised, allowing energy companies to source the cheapest forms of energy. From 1990 to 2001, the average domestic gas bill for standard credit plummeted from £493 to £389 (both 2013 prices). Likewise, in the same period, the average domestic electricity bill on standard credit fell from £424 to £323.[31] Some of this was due to falling world energy prices – but then again, prior to privatisation, electricity companies had been forced to use expensive domestic fuels.

Almost as soon as this process of creating the market was complete, though, politicians set about the task of dismantling it again.

Over the last ten years, the energy market has been successively interfered with through a dizzyingly long list of overlapping initiatives, including, but not limited to, the Climate Change Levy, the Renewables Obligation, the Emissions Trading Scheme, the Climate Change Act 2008, Feed-in Tariffs, the 20-20-20 EU commitment, Electricity Market

Reform, Contracts for Difference, the Capacity Market, the Carbon Price Floor, the Large Combustion Plant Directive and Emissions Performance Standards.

Many of these interventions have been introduced only to tackle problems caused by earlier schemes. Sponsoring intermittent renewables breaks the business model for traditional base power generation, so governments are forced to create a capacity market to subsidise them too.

The net result has been to perform the clever feat of making energy both more expensive and less reliable. The EU's Large Combustion Plant Directive is forcing many of the UK's coal stations to close, removing around 8 GW in capacity.[32] At the same time, all but one of the UK's nuclear power stations is set to shut by 2023. Over the next decade, the UK is set to lose around a quarter, or 20 GW, of its current capacity.[33]

One solution would to be expand nuclear power. For a time, it seemed that 'peak oil' and climate change would make nuclear once again competitive. However, the combination of shale gas and concerns over Fukushima has now caused a second worldwide retreat from nuclear. France, for example, plans to reduce its proportion of electricity generated by nuclear from 80% to 50%, while Germany plans to phase out all its nuclear power by 2022.

In Britain, the plan is to moderately expand capacity. This will be made economic through the government's energy subsidies: in particular, the Contracts for Difference and capacity market. The government intends to bring online 16 GW of capacity by 2030, and in March 2013 planning consent was given for a new nuclear power station at Hinkley Point, Somerset. Four further sites are to be developed by 2030.

Many in the industry have expressed concern that this timetable is overambitious.[34] Other recent nuclear power developments have seen repeated delays. The Finnish Olkiluoto Nuclear Plant, for example, the first to be commissioned in Western Europe in over a decade, has seen its delivery time slip by seven years.[35] The Flamanville reactor in northern France is four years behind schedule.[36] Any similar delays would leave a large gap in Britain's capacity.

As if all this weren't bad enough, the major energy companies now face a two-year-long investigation by the Competition and Markets Authority, which is likely to raise the cost of capital and delay investment decisions. This comes after widespread political unrest about rising energy prices, even though there is little evidence so far that this is due to anti-competitive behaviour by the market participants. In fact, it looks as if global energy prices, combined with environmental policies and exacerbated by regulatory restrictions on tariff structure, are primarily to blame.

It is easy to get confused by this myriad of measures, schemes, interventions and price controls. The government now plans and regulates every aspect of the energy market. Intervention begets intervention, the regulator has become more involved in the operation of the market, and politicians increasingly throw their weight around at the energy companies. We effectively have privatisation in name only. The government tries to plan the balance of future technologies, setting their price and subsiding basic research on top of that. In the case of nuclear, it is often personally negotiating new contracts with foreign suppliers. It has created new markets in carbon or capacity – but, not trusting them, placed hard limits on the price. It has regulated the way energy suppliers contract to each other, and the tariffs they can charge consumers. We do not hide the cost of subsiding food for the poor by adding it to supermarket bills, but we do add the cost of subsidising fuel to energy. On top of this, political posturing over energy bills – where increases have largely been driven by world markets and the policies of governments – is leading to huge uncertainty over the future of the industry.

Spurious justifications are given for this range of interventions, such as 'energy security'. On this point, it should be noted that history, both here and in the US, has shown that government planning of energy and placement in the hands of vested interests has not delivered security before. Coal, for example, can hardly be held up as a good example of energy security in the 1970s.

Almost as long as the list of interventions is the list of fundamental unknowns. Solar power genuinely has the potential to be our main energy source in the future, but we do not know how or when 'grid parity' will be reached. We do not really know how quickly we can build new nuclear power stations, or whether they will run into the persistent delays seen elsewhere. We do not know how much shale gas Britain has access to, whether oil demand will go up or down, or what is the true potential of unconventional sources.

More fundamentally, we know very little about what we are actually trying to achieve. The maths, it turns out, isn't so simple after all. The outputs of economic models of climate change are dominated by the choice of three variables we have very little certainty about: climate sensitivity, the loss function and the discount rate. Climate sensitivity is the degree to which the planet is expected to warm, given higher carbon emissions. As we saw earlier, the IPCC argues that the best estimate for this is between 1.5 and 4.5°C, but it could easily be much lower or higher. Far worse than this is the uncertainty over what the net damage will be from a change in temperature, or how we weigh the interests of current versus future generations.

Combining the uncertainty of energy demand with the uncertainty of the effects of emissions on the climate and the uncertainty of economic growth forecasts means that we know very little of what the ultimate cost of global warming will be. However, for the record, the most recent estimate from the 5th IPCC report suggests that 2.5°C warming would cost the world about 2% of world GDP, or less than a year's growth. This is already much smaller than the high-end forecast of the Stern report that climate change could cost the world 20% of GDP.

Fortunately, the release of the 5th IPCC report represented a new stage in the debate. Compared with past editions, the report was much more humble about its uncertainty, and recognised the importance of adaptation as well as mitigation.

Given the current science, it does not seem likely that climate change will bring about the kind of apocalyptic scenario envisaged in such films as 2004's *The Day after Tomorrow*. It is a real problem, but then the world faces many problems. Even on the worst estimates, climate change is expected to cause less loss of life for another 100 years than the World Health Organization predicts will come from air pollution.

In this scenario, our best insurance policy is a rich economy. It is not a coincidence that the Netherlands finds it easier than Bangladesh to build flood defences. All else being equal, climate change will increase malaria and cut crop yields – but growth has eradicated malaria in the Western world, and African farms could become ten times more efficient with modern techniques.[37]

If we really wanted to commit to cutting emissions to 'lead by example', the most economically efficient way of doing so would be a carbon tax based on an estimate of the social cost of carbon. This would be simple, clear and easy to adjust as new information comes in. This tax could initially be set at a relatively low level, and then gradually raised over time to give households and companies the time to plan and adjust. Arguably, the level of carbon taxes we already pay through fuel or air passenger duty is far too high. The problem would still be, however, that Britain acting alone with a carbon tax would not solve a global problem.

The example of the carbon tax, however, shows us what we should not do. We do not need Green Industrial Policies, renewables obligations, fixing prices and picking winners. Having decided that decarbonisation is the aim, the market should be allowed to devise the cheapest means of achieving it. All these other measures, such as renewables subsidies, are industrial rather than carbon reduction measures, but do not face the same public scrutiny as the subsidies implicit or explicit in other industries because they are wrapped up in the decarbonisation agenda. It's time these subsidies were abolished.

The market will always provide both responsiveness to uncertainty and energy security better than governments. Security of supply is something consumers desire and would be willing to pay for. Suppliers have strong incentives to diversify their sources and technologies against interruptions, because otherwise consumers would desert them. We therefore need less government interference in energy market investment decisions and pricing more broadly, and to return to a situation where the regulator's simple role is regulating natural monopolies and promoting competition. This would help reduce the cost of capital and regulatory uncertainty.

Energy should become a true market again.

THE FREE ENTERPRISE MANIFESTO – ENERGY:

1) We should minimise the barriers to the development of a UK shale gas industry.
2) We should gradually phase out the current system of subsidies for renewable energy.
3) We should increase subsidies and introduce prizes for advances in basic research.
4) We should cut current taxes on carbon to a level consistent with international best estimates of its social cost. As we gain more evidence, we can look to whether these taxes should be further lowered or steadily raised.

6 Crossroads

In the years before the financial crisis, Britain borrowed too much from the rest of the world, running a persistent trade deficit. We need to make it easier for businesses to invest and develop new trade links. Britain should try to expand on the success of London, and seek to become a global hub. We need to turn our attention away from the declining EU, out to the rest of the world and the emerging global middle class. If we can truly become an Enterprise Britain, we have a bright future.

The Two Deficits

In the 1920s, London was the world's largest port, the crossroads of a maritime Empire that spread across the world – but the post-war years were not kind to London's docks. The container revolution in shipping not only catalysed globalisation; it led to bigger ships that could not fit in the East End. Truculent unions and Britain's transition away from manufacturing were to kill them off almost completely. The docklands became an urban wasteland, until their triumphant regeneration in the 1980s. If there is one story that best represents the changes in Britain's economy, it is the decline and transformation of the docklands into the modern financial centre of Canary Wharf.

Today, the ports industry itself is seeing an unexpected comeback. Around forty kilometres to the east of Canary Wharf, the first piers of the new London Gateway opened in 2013. The first new port in Britain for twenty years, it costs its Dubai-based owners DP World £1.5 billion.[1] It is expected to handle 3.5 million containers a year, making it as large as Felixstowe and twice as big again as Southampton.[2] It will create Europe's largest logistic park, and will be capable of docking ships a quarter of a mile long.[3]

The London Gateway is far from alone, however. In recent years, the private sector has spent £2 billion upgrading port capacity in anticipation of future growth.[4] Felixstowe, Bathside Bay, Liverpool, Southampton, Teesport and Bristol have all been granted planning permission to massively expand. Both Felixstowe and Southampton are adding new deep-water berths. The government's official forecasts predict a near-doubling in container demand by the 2030s.[5]

Yet there is a big difference between the ports of today and yesteryear. Whereas Britain's ports once exported its manufactured goods out to the rest of the world, today's super-ports are built for consumer imports. Their speciality is processing the new ultra-large container ships on their way over from Dubai or East Asia. They are built largely to import goods in, not push them out.

In the 1970s, the UK ran trade deficits in goods largely because of its need to import expensive oil. By the early 1980s, as North Sea oil came online, Britain had become a net exporter of oil – but the goods deficit still remained. To further exacerbate matters, since 2005 the UK has once again become a net importer of oil.[6]

Much of this was relatively harmless. While Britain imported goods, it exported services, its speciality. From around 1989 to 1997, the combination of the two, the current account deficit, was gradually shrinking. By 1997, it had reached 0.1% of GDP as measured by the IMF. It was, for all intents and purposes, balanced.

What happened in the next decade was much less harmless. By 2007, the deficit was 2.2% of GDP. In 2013, it was double this again, at 4.5% of GDP.[7]

Why does this matter?

To some, the trade deficit was a sign that Britain could no longer pay its way. In future decades, they worry, even Britain's most advanced industries will eventually be outsourced or undercut by the BRICs (Brazil, Russia, India and China) as they rapidly climb up the value chain. The only way to compete is through a radical 'race to the bottom' on wage costs. Some therefore fear a dystopian Britain, in which an authoritarian government overrides local rights in the name of greater efficiency, and benefits and workers' rights are cut to the bone to drop labour costs.

Rather than accept this unappealing vision, others feel that our best hope is to cling more closely to the safety of the EU. While Britain may be increasingly powerless on its own, the collective might of the EU can 'shelter' us from globalisation. Together, we can tackle the power of increasingly unconstrained multinational corporations, and clamp down on global tax avoidance.

But the good news is that this is largely a false fear. An increasingly prosperous developing world may put extra pressure on us to up our game, but globalisation is more of an opportunity than a threat. Countries are not like companies, having to fear competition that will undercut their livelihood – trade is not a zero-sum game.

What is more, paradoxically, the reason why the trade deficit matters actually has relatively little to do with trade. It was not the falling performance of British firms that saw our trade balance drop, or an 'imbalance' between exports and imports.

It was debt.

Saying we have a trade deficit is just another way of saying we borrowed from abroad. When a household spends more than it earns, we do not usually expect the primary cause to be you getting less good at your job than your peers and seeing your wage drop. What is much more plausible is that you spent more than you could afford, and whacked the difference on a credit card.

The existence of a deficit is not necessarily a bad thing – and, equally, a trade surplus doesn't always signal strength. Japan has run a persistent trade surplus since 1981, and few would claim that its economy was the strongest. Equally, Australia has run a persistent trade deficit for even longer – largely funded by selling attractive homes to rich Chinese families. Just as it can make sense to take on debt to fund your education or buy a house, developing countries often run a deficit as they invest in the capital needed to build new infrastructure.

Unfortunately, none of these excuses really stands up in the case of Britain. From 1995, the household savings ratio declined from 10.3% of income to just 2% in 2008.

There were many reasons for this increase in debt. Perversely, scared by the Asian financial crisis at the end of the 1990s, rather than borrow to invest, many of the developing nations actually became net lenders. In Ben Bernanke's phrase, the world found itself with a global savings glut. At the same time, the UK and US governments ran persistent budget deficits, which in turn sucked in extra borrowing from abroad. Encouraged by booming house prices, home owners increasingly treated their property as an extra credit card.

If all this extra debt had gone on building new productive infrastructure, that would have been one thing. In the private sector, however, restrictive planning laws hampering supply meant that much of it went on a housing bubble. Much of the rest of it went on consumption. Unfortunately, the government was no better – as we have seen, little of the increase in public spending produced measurable improvements.

By the arrival of the financial crisis, the world seemed upside down. You would expect the young, developing East to borrow from the ageing West as it built up its infrastructure. Instead, it was the East that saved, and the West that spent lavishly on consumer goods. In other words, we have been buying goods from China today and promising to pay for them, not in exports today, but in exports tomorrow.

These trends can be reversed. As we have seen, cutting government borrowing and measures to encourage domestic saving would help. But we also have to assess Britain's place in the new globalised world. How can we make globalisation work for us?

The World Is Flat?

The death of distance is nothing new. Writing at the dawn of the steam age in 1839, an English journalist argued that if the progress of the railways were to continue and "distances were thus annihilated, the surface of our country would, as it were, shrivel in size until it became not much bigger than one immense city".

After the trains came the telegraph, the radio, aeroplanes, television, shipping containers and the internet. Today, using the internet, individual teams are increasingly distributed across the world, while supply chains continue to fragment. The archetypal product of today, the iPhone, was conceived in California, runs on a chip designed in Cambridge, uses components from South Korea, Japan and Germany, and is finally constructed in China. Only around 40% of the readership of online newspapers such as *The Guardian* and *The Daily Mail* now comes from the UK.[8] Teenagers grow up watching the same movies, listening to the same music and chatting on the same internet forums.

This applies not just to large multinationals outsourcing their call centres, but to small start-ups too. Working today, an entrepreneur can use the website Kickstarter to raise funds from fans in Tokyo, eLance to locate a designer from Sweden, Alibaba to move their manufacturing to China, and then etsy to sell the final product worldwide. If the product becomes such a success that answering the mail becomes overwhelming, GetFriday will happily provide you with a virtual personal assistant from Bangalore.

But is the world really growing flatter, as journalist Thomas L. Friedman famously suggested in 2005?

In many ways, it is growing spikier as we pack ourselves into ever smaller spaces. Over half the world's population now live in cities, and an extra five million join them every month.[9] In 1950, just three cities contained more than ten million people. By 2025, there will be twenty-seven.[10]

Geography, it turns out, still matters. In the past, cities grew because they were best connected to the trade routes of the world: the merchant cities of Venice and Florence, or the industrial powerhouses of Manchester and New York.

Their strength resulted not just because they formed a convenient crossroads, but because the mingling of peoples and ideas allowed these places to become the first to develop new industries. Many industries work best as hubs. In America, apps and films belong to California, finance and publishing to New York. Taking advantage of these economies of scale, workers end up more productive. In the US, workers in the cities earn 30% more than those who live outside metropolitan areas.[11] Cities, in fact, tend to have more of everything, both good and bad: wages, productivity, patents, crime, disease and poverty.

Cities often confront us with the sharp distinction between rich and poor, living a few streets apart but completely different lives. In both developing and developed countries, however, it is not that cities make people poorer. It is the reverse – cities attract the poor as they seek to become rich.[12] For centuries, people have travelled from countryside to city as they seek to make a new life.

Nowhere, of course, reflects all these trends more than London. In the middle of the century, London suffered from the decline of its traditional manufacturing industries. Its population slumped and crime soared. Today, like its close friend and rival New York, it has made a remarkable comeback. If Britain has transitioned from a manufacturing to an ideas economy, nowhere reflects this change more than the capital.

London is not just surviving globalisation; it is thriving on it. It has become a hub of hubs – a crossroads – for the whole world.

London attracts not just banks and oligarchs, but entertainers and entrepreneurs. Hollywood, for example, has become so dependent on London that its studios are fully booked. While some feared that the end of the 'Harry Potter effect' would leave Britain's film industry shrinking, it is now going from strength to strength. The biggest films of 2015, the new *Star Wars* and *The Avengers*, were both shot in London. While special effects houses are struggling in LA, in Soho they are thriving. Not only was 2013's biggest blockbuster, *Gravity*, shot in Britain, but its effects were created by British company Framestore.

A couple of stops up the Central Line, East London is becoming host to Europe's biggest tech cluster. The number of technology companies in London increased by 76% between 2009 and 2012, creating 27% of the overall growth in jobs.[13] As Debu Purkayastha, a venture capitalist and former Google acquisitions executive, said in a *Financial Times* article, British start-ups can have "the DNA of a consumer-savvy Swedish product manager, an Israeli data manager, a Cambridge or Finnish engineer, [and] a commercially astute London marketer". These start-ups are beginning to be acquired for serious amounts of money. In early 2014, Google bought AI-focused DeepMind for £400 million, while Zynga purchased graphics company NaturalMotion for more than $500 million.[14]

Beyond finance, film and tech, London is equally a world hub for law, fashion, publishing and tourism. Most fundamentally of all, it is a hub for the world's peoples, containing fifty communities of over 10,000 people, speaking over 300 different languages and practicing fourteen major religions. As of 2013, London is the world's most visited city.[15] London is the richest of the 271 official European regions,[16] and measured per capita, the fifth richest city in the world.[17] On nearly every ranking of world power or influence, London is either number one or shortly behind New York.[18]

London has become so successful that many worry it is starting to leave the rest of the UK behind. Londoners earn on average around a third more than the rest of Britain, are four times more likely to have been born abroad and are significantly more likely to have a degree.[19]

Has this success been bought by 'draining the life' from the economy? Should we try to rebalance the economy towards the north?

It is true that Britain, like France, is unusually dependent on a single city. This is, of course, far from a new complaint. It was exactly this idea that led post-war politicians to try to constrain the growth of

London – which not only did nothing to improve the lot of deprived areas, but severely undercut London for a generation.

London's success has been organic and unplanned – we are still not sure why it has made such a comeback. Regional policy did not fail in the post-war era because politicians were incompetent or unlucky. Nor is London 'unfairly' advantaged through greater infrastructure investment. Turning around a city is just a very hard thing to do – worldwide, government attempts to revitalise cities such as Detroit through infrastructure investment have consistently failed.[20]

At present, London subsidises the rest of the country by about £15 billion a year. Ultimately, we should adopt General Motors' famous slogan about America: what is good for London is good for Britain. Having the world's leading city is an asset we should be proud about, rather than frightened of. Moreover, it is an asset we have not yet fully taken advantage of.

For London has been so successful that it is now increasingly running up against constraints. More to the point, these constraints aren't the natural limits of geography or diminishing returns, but largely artificial and human. If we want to ensure its position as the twenty-first century hub, we need to ease the pressure in three crucial areas: planning, immigration and transport.

After all, by far the easiest way for any business to increase revenues is to stop turning willing customers away.

Take again the example of film. Space is so limited that the new UK set series of 24 found itself having to work out of a converted warehouse. For seven years, the UK's leading film studio Pinewood has been trying to expand, converting a former landfill site next to the M25 into a new backlot, with settings from a medieval castle to modern New York. This would allow it not only to host more blockbusters, but also to create a significant number of jobs and new homes.

Despite the obvious shortage, and the opportunity to build on a modern British success story, the expansion of Pinewood was blocked three times over, with approval only finally coming in 2014 after the intervention of the secretary of state. Local opposition group *Stop Project Pinewood* argued, somewhat contradictorily, that the project was unlikely to make much of a difference as Pinewood was only a small part of the film industry – but if it did go ahead, it would risk turning Pinewood into a monopoly "to the detriment of other smaller studios".[21] This is an unusual level of concern for the multinational Time Warner corporation. The local council's views were hardly more coherent. They worried that expanding the region's principal industry would have a "harmful impact on the character of the area".[22]

Britain can cope without producing more films. But the effect of planning laws bite right across the economy. They make it harder for new businesses to start or expand, and ultimately increase consumer prices on the high street while decreasing choice. Britain has six of the world's fifty most expensive cities for commercial space, with Manchester costing more than Manhattan. Our planning laws are one significant reason why land-intensive industries such as manufacturing declined so rapidly in Britain. A hectare of agricultural land costs £20,000 in Oxfordshire, while a hectare with permission for industrial development goes for closer to £1 million.[23]

But the biggest cost of our planning laws is, of course, housing. Nowhere is this truer than in London and the surrounding South East. The same £20,000 hectare of farmland would be worth £4 million if it came with permission to build new homes.

The 1947 Town and Country Planning Act effectively nationalised decisions over land planning. The level of private house building has never recovered. In 2012, construction started on just 107,000 new homes in Britain, under a third of the number seen in the 1930s. Official estimates suggest that we need to build an annual 232,000 houses just to keep up with demand. London alone is expected to see a million new residents over the next decades. Those homes that are built are much smaller, roughly half the size of a new pre-war home.[24]

The inevitable consequence of a shortage in supply has been ever higher prices. Over the last forty years, British house prices have increased by a factor of forty, compared with a twelvefold increase in general inflation. In most English-speaking countries, the average house costs three times your salary. In large parts of England, it is closer to seven times.[25]

The negative impacts this creates for the economy are legion. It drives up welfare bills, with the total cost of housing benefit in real terms quadrupling over the last three decades.[26] One in five households are in receipt of housing benefit, and 44% of renters.[27] It redistributes huge amounts of money from renters to owners, and from young to old. It makes it much harder for families to move in pursuit of a new job. It encourages people to use their house as their principal means of 'saving', and exacerbates the instability of the business cycle and general financial instability. It leads to increased tensions over immigration and prices poorer families out of the catchment area of good schools. It was a significant factor behind the rise in personal debt over the last twenty years, and the fall in the savings ratio.

Ultimately, we need to build more homes. Britain already has the highest property taxes in the developed world, twice the OECD average,[28] and it has yet to bring demand significantly down. This cannot all come from brownfield land – London has enough for just 30,000 new homes[29] – or forcing builders to give up land banks faster.

Fortunately, we have plenty of space. Nobody anywhere wants to concrete over the whole of England's countryside. 'Countryside vs. development' is a false dilemma. Only 2.3% of England has been 'concreted over', and 6–10% developed in general. Converting the use of just 2% of our land would give room to create an additional eight million homes.[30] Even if this were not the case, we could easily ease the restrictions on building height. We are unlikely to run out of room in the sky anytime soon.

That said, equally, we cannot just build anywhere with no respect for local residents' rights. Most people bought their home because they liked the area, the atmosphere and the view. It is unfair to swamp them with new neighbours without their consent, or to let their house value collapse. So-called NIMBYs (Not In My Back Yard) are not always being unreasonable. Housing developments have, in the jargon, externalities.

One way to solve this conflict is to give the government the final say. This was the approach taken in 1947. Local councils were given the power to create 'plans' for the development of their land, and veto anything they disapproved of. Needless to say, this has not worked very well.

Even putting aside its negative impact on housing supply, the planning system has had numerous side effects. The planning system has led local officials to effectively try to plan their local economy, setting down restrictions and regulations on the number of parking spaces, downstairs toilets or the type and texture of tarmac to use. All too often development finds itself blocked if it doesn't fit with the fashionable trend of the day: limiting car use, encouraging green manufacturing or affordable homes. Even if they had the knowledge to do this sensibly, it should not be an urban planner's job to dictate what type of society we are to have. Inevitably, given their complexity and the intrusion of politics, planning decisions are achingly slow, taking on average around 98 weeks.[31]

We should remove all restrictions on development that don't directly affect anyone else. Especially on brownfield land, there should be a presumption that you can do whatever you like with your own property. If you wish to convert commercial space into housing, there is no real economic justification for the government stopping you.

Fortunately, even on greenfield land, there are many ways of giving communities a say without going all the way towards today's full command-and-control economy. Today's planning system only gives very limited and indirect compensation to local residents. It is as likely to get funnelled into the pet projects of the council as to ensure the new project is a win-win for everyone.

One possibility would be the radical expansion of the Garden Cities model. Each city would be developed by a single private corporation, allowing it to internalise many of the externalities – it would have to pay for new transport links, but would then get to profit from the increased value this creates in the value of the new homes. After the developer has set out its suggested rate of compensation, the affected residents could be given a direct referendum on whether they approve of the project.

We could also expand existing towns through innovative compensation mechanisms such as community land auctions.[32] Under this system, owners of land would first state the amount they were willing to sell for. The local council would aggregate the various bids, and decide which land it wishes to allow development on. It would then hold a second auction for developers to purchase this land. The advantage of this system is that it maximises councils' share of the profits from granting planning permission – giving them both the incentive to do so and the financial ability to make sure locals are better off. Of course, this could also be achieved with a greater degree of fiscal decentralisation, as outlined earlier in the book.

Allowing more development, especially in housing, is not just a matter of increasing the size of the economy; it's also about making life better for our current young population. Many currently fear that they will never be able to own their own home.

But there's another reason why we have to be ready for new development: because demand for the things that Britain is good at is about to explode.

Looking East

For much of the twentieth century, the world's economic centre of gravity hung somewhere over the Norwegian Sea, just north of the UK. From around 1500 to 1950, it had gradually shifted west, attracted by the growing power of the North American economy. Now, it is moving east, and fast. According to McKinsey, between 2000 and 2010 it moved at the fastest rate in history. Every year, it moved around 140 km closer to China – it is now hovering somewhere over the middle of Russia.[33]

The first phase of globalisation has been the most effective anti-poverty programme in history. Largely driven by the expansion of markets, trade and free enterprise ideas, it has seen one billion lifted out of sheer, horrific, absolute poverty as developing countries catch up.

To its critics, however, globalisation has always had a dark side. They argue that mass outsourcing has stolen jobs from the Western world and undercut the wages of the working class. Free trade may benefit the country as a whole, and the better-off in particular, but on this view it is a disaster for the low-skilled. Furthermore, so the argument goes, it is exploitative of those in the developing world.

Whether you buy this argument or not, what has been largely unnoticed by its critics is that this first phase of globalisation is now coming to an end. Whatever downsides to globalisation there might have once been for Britain, they are now largely over. Globalisation is almost entirely an uncomplicated plus from here on out.

The first phase of globalisation saw manufacturing jobs move to low-wage Asian countries. This had two opposite effects for workers in Britain: bringing significantly cheaper goods, but also taking away many traditional jobs. While this process is still going on as new low-cost regions such as Africa come online, this is likely to have little impact on jobs in the West. Most of the jobs that could be outsourced have already gone. A British worker today is far more likely to lose his job to a robot than an Asian. Indeed, the cost advantages of automation mean than in some cases outsourcing is going into reverse.

An increasing number of Western companies are starting to 're-shore' production back to their home country.

But even more important than the supply is the demand side. The poor, almost by definition, cannot afford to splash out on many luxuries. As they get richer, however, they will increasingly look for new ways to entertain themselves.

By 2030, the global middle class is expected to more than double, from 2.5 billion today to 4.9 billion.[34] McKinsey predicts that many of these consumers will be based in new mega-cities. In the three years from 2007 to 2010, China saw the appearance of a new city with a population above ten million each year. By 2025, they forecast that 440 cities in emerging markets will contain one billion new consumers, generating half of world GDP growth and spending $10 trillion a year. For the first time, the majority of the world will be able to enjoy something closer to a Western standard of living.

If there is one country that should be able to benefit from this expanded market, it is Britain. Over the course of its history, Britain has exported its language and tastes to every corner of the globe. In future years, an extra two billion people will add to the markets for watching Premiership football, drinking Scotch whiskey or reading about boy wizards. It is difficult to think of a better opportunity for a largely service-based economy specialising in financial services, management and business services, with significant high-value-added manufacturing and creative industries, speaking English and in a roughly optimal time-zone.

Unfortunately, even the best opportunities can be squandered.

In the last chapter of this book, our self-defeating approach to energy policy was highlighted. Equally important, however, is how both Britain's horizons and its trade remain overly dominated by Europe. When Britain first joined the European Economic Community in 1973, it was seen as a way of expanding trade. Today, the EU is unfortunately just as likely to restrict trade as encourage it. In the short term, Britain's overdependence on Europe led to its economy being dragged down by the Eurozone crisis. In the long term, European regulation creates increasing obstacles to British business. It is estimated that cutting the cost of EU social regulations by 50% could result in a boost to economic output equivalent to the creation of 140,000 new jobs in the UK.[35] Moreover, being part of the EU stops us signing free trade deals with other nations. While talks between the EU and the US on the Transatlantic Trade and Investment Partnership have hit rocky ground, Iceland (with a population of just 315,000) has agreed a free trade agreement with China.[36]

As Jim O'Neill, coiner of the 'BRICs' acronym, argued, the trade-off between Europe and the emerging world is becoming "less clear than it used to be". He believes that we cannot 'afford' to squander these opportunities as a result of "decisions that may be taken to ensure the United States of Europe".[37] Today, trade with BRICs makes up only around 5% of our total exports.[38]

The inevitable logic of the euro is driving its member countries ever closer to pooling their sovereignty. It is as yet unclear whether we will be able to find a two-track solution that preserves the rights of non-euro countries such as the UK.

Whether Britain chooses to remain a member of the EU or not, Britain hardly needs to fear irrelevance on the world stage. Given its high birth rate, it is projected to have the largest population in Europe by 2050. It will remain one of the world's richest and most connected economies. The Transatlantic Trade and Investment Partnership offers the possibility of a free trade zone far bigger than Europe alone, which an independent Britain could easily join. Besides, it is not as if 'pooling' our influence in Europe has been a huge success. The EU's supposed lead on climate change has largely been ignored by the rest of the world, while few would rely on it rather than NATO as their first line of military defence.

Expanding into new markets does not happen automatically, however. It depends crucially on relationships and well-worn trade routes. Even in an increasingly digital economy, the best video conference solution is as yet no substitute for a firm handshake.

Ever since its foundation by the Romans as Londinium, Britain's capital has made its living as a port. Once it sold its wares by sea. Today, London's businessmen travel by air. London is still arguably the best-connected business city in the world. While the new London Gateway may decrease the cost of imports to the city, it is Heathrow, Gatwick and Stansted that will allow it to earn its living in the future. Between them, London's five airports offer access to around 350 international destinations.[39] In one survey for London First, 90% of respondents argued that growing the number of international air links was crucial to the long-term health of London and their business.[40] Forty per cent of the UK's exports, measured by value, go by air.[41]

However, this advantage is already starting to slip. Little flexibility remains to start new speculative routes to the expanding cities of the emerging world. Heathrow's two runways now run at nearly 99% capacity.[42] During peak periods, aeroplanes can often be held circling at Heathrow for up to 45 minutes.[43] An airport that was originally designed to cope with a maximum of fifty million passengers now sees over sixty million pass through each year.[44] Gatwick operates at 95% capacity, and is considered the busiest single-runway airport in the world.

In the last twenty years, Heathrow has fallen from first in Europe to fifth in terms of destinations served.[45] Heathrow's route network has already dropped from 227 destinations in 1990 to 180 now, and is forecast to drop to 147.[46] Paris and Frankfurt offer 1,000 more annual flights to the three largest cities in China than Heathrow. Heathrow misses out on at least twenty-one emerging market destinations that are served by daily flights to and from its European rivals.[47] The UK is already missing out on the new tourism boom from the emerging Chinese middle class. Earnings from tourism grew by 85.6% in Germany from 2000 to 2010, compared with only 37.4% in the UK.[48]

Compare the situation of London with Dubai. In recent decades, Dubai has sought to transition from short-term oil wealth to long-term prosperity by turning itself into a central hub for the Middle East and Africa. Dubai sees itself as the centre of a new Silk Road, connecting together Asia and Europe. More than half the world's population, 3.5 billion people, live within the reach of an eight-hour flight. Air traffic has tripled in the last decade.[49] Recognising that its current two-runway airport is running out of space, Dubai is investing in the construction of a new facility. The Al Maktoum International airport will be ten times as big again as the current Dubai International Airport and Dubai Cargo village combined. Its five runways will allow up to four aircraft to land simultaneously, twenty-four hours a day.

While Heathrow has been forbidden a third runway, Frankfurt has just opened its fourth to match Paris Charles de Gaulle, and Amsterdam Schiphol has six. Further afield, the world's biggest airport, Atlanta, already has five runways. The second and third, Chicago O'Hara and Dallas Fort Worth, have seven each. In 2015, China plans to open a new nine-runway airport, Beijing Daxing International, serving 370,000 passengers a day.[50]

How much extra space is London likely to need? Between 1980 and 2005, aviation demand grew by around 6% a year. The Department for Transport has judged that growth is now likely to slow to 1–3% as oil prices increase and low-cost airlines run out of scope to cut costs. The recent Howard Davies' Airport Commission argued that if there were no constraints, the number of passengers would more than double to 450 million terminal passengers a year (mppa), with the final number having a 60% chance of being between 380 to 530 mppa. (For reference, the UK saw 211 mppa in 2011.) The Commission judges that without further capacity, Heathrow became full in 2010, and Gatwick will be full in 2020, Luton in 2030 and Stansted in 2041. The gap between demand and capacity would be around 200,000 air transport movements in 2050, or the equivalent of an extra runway. After 2050, demand would continue to grow, requiring a second new runway. The Commission's economic model suggests that over sixty years the shortage of capacity would cost the aviation industry around £20 billion and the wider economy £40 billion.

However, even those forecasts look extremely conservative, representing a historically dramatic slowing of demand. World oil prices could fall as easily as rise, or lower than expected climate sensitivity and better technology could lead to a lower carbon price. The earlier 2003 White Paper believed that we might reach 500 mppa by 2030. While the recession may have set us back a few years, it is difficult to believe that much else has fundamentally changed. Even with its low forecasts of demand, the Commission notes that a three-runway Heathrow would be at 80–90% capacity again by 2030.

If Britain is to build long-lasting connections with emerging markets, it will need good transport links. Inevitably, these transport links will initially be speculative – which means that they will not happen if airports and airlines do not have the opportunity to take a risk. Given that private companies will be bearing the risk and cost, it is better for Britain to have more aviation capacity than we need than to see our economy artificially limited.

To really build relationships with other nations, however, we will need some of those who visit to be more than short-term guests.

London has always been a cosmopolitan home to new waves of immigrants, from silk-weaving Huguenots settling in Spitalfields to the arrival of the first post-war Caribbeans on the *Empire Windrush*. As far back as the early eighteenth century, Voltaire noted that in the Exchange of London one could find "the Jew, the Mahometan and the Christian [dealing] with one another as if they were of the same religion.... There are thirty [religions in England], and they live happily together in peace."[51]

Nobody doubts the importance of immigrants to London's economy. Around 40% of the city's residents were born abroad. Given their bravery in moving to a new land, it is no surprise that immigrants tend to be more entrepreneurial. Some reports suggest that one in seven British companies were started by an immigrant.[52] This global sharing of talent is good for everyone. In the US, where would tech titans like Google be without Russian immigrant Sergey Brin, or, for that matter, Apple without the contribution of British chief designer Jonathan Ive?

Yet there has been considerable concern about the impact of accelerated immigration on the low-paid over the past decade. While it is a fallacy to think of a fixed number of jobs in an economy, it is certainly theoretically possible for immigration to cut the wages of the lowest-skilled. Increased supply, all else being equal, normally lowers prices. Of course, all else is not equal, and the empirical evidence for lower wages from increased immigration is remarkably modest – although some studies find it depresses wages for the bottom fifth of Britons.[53]

More to the point, the larger worries come from the non-economic impacts of immigration. In a perfect world, public services and housing might be able to rapidly expand to meet increased demand. Nobody, after all, worries that Wetherspoons or Primark will not be able to deal with an influx of new customers.

In reality, however, public services are unlikely to ever be as responsive or efficient as the private sector. A rapid increase in population is likely to lead to shortages and queues. More nebulously, it takes time for a culture to absorb new arrivals. A Britain that absorbs five million newcomers a year is unlikely to look much like Britain for long. This can lead to resentment among local people, who feel that they are being queue-jumped by new arrivals, while seeing their communities change.

Advocates of completely open borders will claim that these are challenges posed because of the existence of the welfare state and government regulations, not immigration per se. It's certainly true that planning law liberalisation and restrictions on welfare are more targeted solutions to some of the problems identified. Ultimately, though, there will always be a need to provide public goods, and as such we need some degree of 'management' of migration.

At present, Britain has a schizophrenic immigration system. We enjoy open borders with the EU, while setting strict limits on those from elsewhere. This is, at best, inconsistent.

Unfortunately, the government is unlikely to be any better at judging the future employment needs of the economy than it is at picking winners in any other areas of the economy. At the other extreme, a first-come first-served approach is unlikely to be the most efficient use of a limited number of immigration spaces.

Perhaps the easiest way of solving this dilemma would be to sell a new class of immigration visas to companies or individuals. This would allow the private economy to prioritise where workers were needed. Given that newcomers would already have paid their entrance fee, nobody could complain that they were seeking to scrounge off the welfare state. Immigration would become much less controversial – high-skilled immigration would no longer face today's bureaucratic barriers, while British natives would be unlikely to find themselves undercut. There would be no danger of unconstrained immigration undermining British culture. If levels of immigration became too high, government could dampen the flow through increasing the price. Equally, if we felt there was space for more newcomers, the price could be dropped.

This absolutely does not mean that immigration should only be available to the rich. Just as with higher education, a loan system should be set up to allow individuals to pay off the cost of their visa over time. Equally, governments and charities could provide scholarships to fund other visas for humanitarian reasons.

A high interest in coming to the UK should ultimately be seen as a sign of economic success rather than weakness. More sensible systems of planning and immigration would substantially assist in defusing the debate and the key pressure points caused by immigration. But if we really want to succeed in a globalised world, we need to create the conditions for enterprise too.

Enterprise Britain

In just over thirty years, the small fishing village of Shenzhen in China has been transformed into a modern metropolis. Between 1979 and 2005, the GDP of the city grew from 1.96 million RMB to 500 billion RMB (around £35 billion).[54] The city now has a population of around twelve million workers[55] and seventeen sea, land and air ports.[56]

Shenzhen has become a global hub for manufacturing, particularly in electronics. It is the home of the infamous Foxconn, the manufacturer of Apple's products. Most of the world's largest technology brands have outsourced significant proportions of their manufacturing and assembly to the city's factories.

When most people think of Shenzhen, they picture sweatshop labour. This is unfair. While Shenzhen may initially have benefited from its cheap labour costs, wages are now rising significantly faster than productivity. Other developing countries, such as Vietnam or inland areas of China, are now far cheaper.[57] On the other hand, none of these locations can match Shenzhen's depth and breadth of suppliers. Shenzhen's comparative advantage is better understood now as resulting from its greater economies of scale, rather than cheap labour.

Shenzhen served an important political, as well as economic, function. Deliberately located far away from Beijing, the new Special Economic Zone allowed the government to experiment with radical policies, cutting taxes and regulation. In 1984 similar reforms were spread to fourteen coastal cities, and by 1994 to much of the country. Together, these reforms have created the fastest and most significant reduction in poverty in world history.

The Chinese government is now looking to encourage the next stage of the country's economic development by creating, in effect, a Shenzhen within Shenzhen. A new area in the city has been earmarked to experiment with policies aimed at attracting service industries, including a 15% rate of corporation tax and exempting workers in finance, legal services or creative industries from income tax.[58]

Shenzhen did not come out of a vacuum. Enterprise Zones descend from the much older institution of free ports. In medieval times, Amsterdam's entrepôt allowed it to dominate European trade. Later free ports included Gibraltar (from 1704) and Singapore (from 1819).

But the real role model for China, and its leader Deng Xiaoping in the 1980s, was Hong Kong. Over the course of the twentieth century, the British colony achieved remarkable success. Real GDP per capita increased eight times between 1913 and 1980, and the average citizen was ten times as rich as the mainland Chinese.[59] By 1987, the residents of Hong Kong were richer than the British, and today they are 40% wealthier.[60]

Other countries have adopted the Enterprise Zone model. According to the World Bank, there are now approximately 3,000 Special Economic Zones in 135 countries, creating about $500 billion in value.[61]

In the 1970s Dubai built Jebel Ali Port, aiming to create the largest port in the Middle East. In the 1980s, the state went further, and created the Jebel Ali Free Zone. The zone has become a significant distribution and logistics centre, responsible for 30% of Dubai's GDP.[62] The government has replicated the model in 32 free zones[63] across the UAE: for example, the new Internet City and Media City. Dubai, in general, has very low taxation: there are no income taxes, and, in practice, only energy companies pay corporate taxation. The free zones go still further, allowing 100% foreign ownership, and offering zero custom duties or quotas, no controls on capital movement, and reductions in red tape and regulation.

Britain, too, has unleased two waves of enterprise. In the 1970s, inspired by the success of Hong Kong and Singapore, urban planning expert Peter Hall argued that Britain should try to emulate their model. He believed that by lowering tax and reducing regulation, "fairly shameless free enterprise", the economic prospects of deprived areas could be significantly improved.[64] At the 1980 budget, Chancellor Geoffrey Howe announced Britain's Enterprise Zone policy. In total, 38 zones were created between 1981 and 1996. Later, in 2011, George Osborne announced the creation of twenty-four new Enterprise Zones across England. The Scottish government has announced its own four Enterprise Areas, while Wales is planning seven Enterprise Zones.

Enterprise Zones have their place. As the example of Shenzhen shows, they can serve as laboratories for radical policies, demonstrating the benefit of lower taxes and regulation. When they are situated in the right location, as at Canary Wharf, they can transform the economic landscape.

They do, however, require the government to have the wisdom to choose that location, and to choose cold economic logic over politics and special interests. There is always the fear that, as well as creating new companies and wealth, they will simply suck them in from elsewhere in a zero-sum competition.

What if, instead of creating small, sporadic pockets of free enterprise, we instead decided to turn the whole of Britain into one great Enterprise Nation? What would this look like?

To start with, it would need low business taxes. Just as Enterprise Zones attract new investment through lower rates of corporation tax, Britain should seek as a nation to have one of the lowest rates.

This is sometimes depicted by countries with relatively high rates as unfair competition. They worry about a global 'race to the bottom' in tax rates. This is looking at the issue the wrong way around. Global tax competition may very well drive all states to become as efficient and attractive to business as possible to justify their tax rates – but this surely benefits everyone.

In the ideal tax system, as described by many economists, you would pay tax once, when you spend your income on consumption. In reality, most tax systems penalise saving and investment, taxing some sources of income many times over. Moreover, they give a significant tax advantage to cost of debt interest, rather than equity sharing of risk. Is it so surprising that many Western economies save too little and borrow too much?

It is no longer controversial to point out that corporation tax is the most harmful tax for the economy. In the most extreme scenario, if tax competition drove the tax to zero, the world would likely be better off. As the OECD puts it, "corporate taxes are the most harmful type of tax for economic growth ... [65] They are ultimately borne by individuals – by shareholders [through lower returns] ... by the labour force through lower wages and/or by consumers through higher prices ... In small open economies the corporate income tax is borne, to a large extent, by labour and consumers."[66]

The recent Mirrlees Review of the tax system concluded that "the standard corporate income tax is likely to distort company behaviour in several ways ... Borrowing is favoured over retained profits or new equity as a source of finance for corporate investment, leaving firms more exposed to the risk of bankruptcy ... The corporate income tax increases the cost of capital and reduces investment."[67]

Globalisation, the internet and e-commerce have transformed the way businesses are operated. Businesses used to operate within borders – they now increasingly operate without borders. International tax law has not kept up to date with the pace of change, meaning that national corporation tax bases have steadily been eroded over time. Often, there are no good answers as how to allocate costs and profits between a multinational's different territories. However, it is simply not fair for UK firms to be left paying a 20% rate while large foreign-based multinationals avoid corporation taxes on an industrial scale.

Already, the average global corporation tax has fallen consecutively in the last eleven years, from 29.03% in 2000 to 22.96% in 2011.[68] Britain has to cut its rates just to remain competitive. Already we have gone from the third lowest rate in the EU to the fourteenth.

The Coalition government has brought the main rate of corporation tax down to 20% over the course of the parliament of 2010–2015. We should aim, however, for a headline rate of 10%. Much of this could be paid for by the elimination of the current allowances and reliefs. This would create a simpler, lower rate, suitable for the globalised, internet age.

Corporation tax should be the start, but it should not be the end of our tax simplification agenda. Just as corporation tax is unfair to domestic over foreign firms, business rates favour internet companies over those on the high street. We should slowly seek to lower them. Under many economic models, the optimal rate of capital taxation for both workers and capitalists is zero. Air passenger duty (APD) discourages foreign businessmen and tourists from visiting us, while aviation carbon emissions are now covered by the EU Emissions Trading Scheme. APD is so damaging to the economy, in fact, that one estimate suggests abolishing it would pay for itself in faster growth. Why not give it a go? According to the Institute for Fiscal Studies' Mirrlees Report, "there is no sound case for maintaining stamp duty and we believe that it should be abolished".[69]

In order to afford these tax cuts, however, we will have to have an affordable state. The reforms suggested in this book therefore go together, as outlined below.

In an Enterprise Britain, a slimmed-down government will focus on only what it can do best, leaving the rest to the private sector. In order to tackle an ageing population and the cost pressures of the welfare state, the government will need the innovation of a start-up and a combined welfare and tax system that encourages work and enterprise. By freeing up the universities and lowering the regulatory barriers to competition, Enterprise Britain will have the best chance of creating the industries of the future. Instead of an industrial policy seeking to return us to the past, protecting inefficient companies behind trade barriers, we would become a crossroads for the world once more.

An Enterprise Britain would be able to deal with our worries about the future. There would be no divide between an innovative private sector and a stagnant public sector, so increased automation would benefit everyone. The return of a savings and work culture would ensure that an ageing population remained affordable. Climate change would be tackled not by expensive top-down plans, but by the development of new technology. The rises of places like Shenzhen in our new globalised age would represent not competition to be afraid of, but over a billion new consumers to sell to.

But an Enterprise Britain would not just be about greater efficiency or more money. It would be a happier place to live. Britain would be a confident country, more relaxed in itself. It would earn its future through creativity and trade, not just working ever longer hours. It would be a more equal country, too, as the benefits of new technology created more shared prosperity than any minor change to benefits ever could. It would be genuinely greener, rather than simply exporting our pollution to poorer nations. We would be a cosmopolitan and creative country, open to the world and learning from the best. A dynamic public service would deliver real improvements to our education and health, but leave us free to choose our own way of life. We would, in short, be richer.

One of the biggest mistakes in politics and policy making is to assume that there is a set path; that history is predetermined. This book has highlighted some of the largest challenges Britain is likely to face in the coming decades, but there will no doubt be 'unknown unknowns' which crop up to interrupt these predictions. But with the right policies, based around the flexibility, innovativeness and openness offered by being a liberal market economy, there is no reason why Britain should not both meet these challenges and excel in the coming decades. The doom-mongers are wrong. Britain's best days are ahead. It's now time to create the conditions so that we can fulfil our potential.

THE FREE ENTERPRISE MANIFESTO – TRADE:

1) We should seek to retain London's position as a world leader by making it easier for private developers to build new housing and aviation capacity.
2) We should introduce a new system of market-based immigration visas.
3) We should seek to renegotiate EU treaties in order to reduce the burden of labour regulation, among other things.
4) We should lower the headline rate of corporation tax to 10% and phase out other damaging business taxes.

Notes

Introduction

1. Angus Burgin, *The Great Persuasion: Reinventing Free Markets since the Depression* (Cambridge, MA: Harvard University Press, 2012); Eric Hobsbawm, *The Age of Extremes* (Harmondsworth: Penguin, 1994), p. 94.
2. Author calculations derived from Sally Hills, Ryland Thomas, and Nicholas Dimsdale, The UK Recession in Context – What Do Three Centuries of Data Tell Us?, *Bank of England Quarterly*, Q4 (2010).
3. Will Hutton, A Short History of Capitalism's Rise and Fall, *The Observer*, 5 October 2008, http://www.theguardian.com/business/2008/oct/05/credit-crunch.marketturmoil1 (accessed 31 December 2014).
4. Will Hutton, This Terrifying Moment Is Our One Chance for a New World, *The Observer*, 5 October 2008, http://www.theguardian.com/business/2008/oct/05/banks.marketturmoil (accessed 31 December 2014).
5. Larry Elliot, George Osborne's Welfare Cuts Pander to the Distortions of Benefits Street, *The Guardian*, 12 January 2014, http://www.theguardian.com/business/economics-blog/2014/jan/12/george-osborne-welfare-cuts-distortions-benefits-street (accessed 31 December 2014).
6. 1945 Labour Party Election Manifesto, http://www.labour-party.org.uk/manifestos/1945/1945-labour-manifesto.shtml (accessed 31 December 2014).
7. 1945 Conservative Party General Election Manifesto, http://www.conservative-party.net/manifestos/1945/1945-conservative-manifesto.shtml (accessed 31 December 2014).
8. Ben S. Bernanke, The Macroeconomics of the Great Depression: A Comparative Approach, *Journal of Money, Credit and Banking*, Vol. 27, No. 1 (February 1995).
9. The Economy Report (15 August 1931), John Maynard Keynes, *Essays in Persuasion* (New York: W.W.Norton, 2009 [1963]), p. 90.
10. Hills, Thomas, and Dimsdale, The UK Recession in Context.
11. George Trefgarne, *Metroboom: Lessons from Britain's Recovery in the 1930s* (London: CPS, 2012), p. 23.
12. Barry Eichengreen, The British Economy between the Wars, in Roderick Floud and Paul Johnson (eds), *The Cambridge Economic History of Modern Britain, Vol II: Economic Maturity, 1860–1939* (Cambridge: Cambridge University Press, 2004), p. 35.
13. Nicholas Crafts, British Relative Economic Decline Revisited: The Role of Competition, *Explorations in Economic History* Vol. 49, No. 1 (2012).
14. Scott Sumner, The Unacknowledged Success of Neoliberalism, Econlib, http://www.econlib.org/library/Columns/y2010/Sumnerneoliberalism.html (accessed 31 December 2014).

15. Author calculations derived from The Conference Board Total Economy Database, Output, Labor and Labor Productivity Country Details, 1950–2014, January 2014.

16. Stewart Wood, The God That Failed, *New Statesman*, 29 September 2011, http://www.newstatesman.com/uk-politics/2011/09/neoliberalism-essay-work (accessed 31 December 2014).

17. Matt Ridley, *The Rational Optimist* (New York: HarperCollins, 2010).

18. Jonathan Haidt, *The Righteous Mind: Why Good People Are Divided by Politics and Religion* (New York: Vintage, 2012).

19. Paul H. Rubin, *Folk Economics* (New York: Routledge, 2002).

20. Megan McArdle, *The Up Side of Down: Why Failing Well Is the Key to Success* (New York: Penguin, 2014), Kindle location 585.

21. Don Coursey, Experimental Economics, *The Concise Encyclopaedia of Economics*, http://www.econlib.org/library/Enc/ExperimentalEconomics.html (accessed 31 December 2014).

22. Ridley, *The Rational Optimist*, p. 117.

23. Jim Giles, Internet Encyclopaedias Go Head to Head, *Nature*, 438 (2005), 900–901.

24. According to the top sites on Alexa, http://www.alexa.com/topsites, on 21 April 2014, Reddit is the 58th most visited site on the internet, while Nytimes.com is 127th. (The BBC is 64th and the *Daily Mail* 95th.)

25. Katherine Boyle, Yes, Kickstarter Raises More Money for Artists Than the NEA. Here's Why That's Not Really Surprising, 7 July 2013, *Washington Post*, http://www.washingtonpost.com/blogs/wonkblog/wp/2013/07/07/yes-kickstarter-raises-more-money-for-artists-than-the-nea-heres-why-thats-not-really-surprising/ (accessed 31 December 2014).

26. Jim Manzi, *Uncontrolled: The Surprising Payoff of Trial-and-Error for Business, Politics, and Society* (New York: Basic Books, 2012); Arnold Kling, Macroeconometrics: The Science of Hubris, *Critical Review*, Vol. 23, No. 1–2 (2011).

27. Tom Steiner and John Davis, Nasty, Brutish, Short: Why Businesses Prosper Then Die at an Ever Faster Pace, *City A.M.*, 10 February 2014, http://www.cityam.com/article/1392004929/nasty-brutish-short-why-businesses-prosper-then-die-ever-faster-pace (accessed 31 December 2014).

28. Author calculations derived from J. Bolt, and J. L. van Zanden, The First Update of the Maddison Project; Re-Estimating Growth before 1820, Maddison Project Working Paper 4, 2013, http://www.ggdc.net/maddison/maddison-project/data.htm; *World Economic Outlook* (Washington DC: IMF, April 2014).

29. Joe Hicks and Grahame Allen, A Century of Change: Trends in UK Statistics since 1900, House of Commons Library Research Paper 99/111, 1999.

30. ONS, 170 Years of Industrial Change across England and Wales, 2011, http://www.ons.gov.uk/ons/rel/census/2011-census-analysis/170-years-of-industry/170-years-of-industrial-changeponent.html (accessed 31 December 2014).

31. Deidre McCloskey, Factual Free-Market Fairness, 2012, http://bleeding-heartlibertarians.com/2012/06/factual-free-market-fairness/ (accessed 31 December 2014).

32. Steven Pinker, *The Better Angels of Our Nature* (New York: Viking, 2011), p. 63.

33. Carl Benedikt Frey and Michael A. Osborne, The Future of Employment: How Susceptible Are Jobs to Computerisation?, 2013, http://www.oxfordmartin.ox.ac.uk/downloads/academic/The_Future_of_Employment.pdf (accessed 31 December 2014).

34. Author calculation derived from ONS, House Price Index, Table 22, mix-adjusted index, February 2014.

35. Mark Easton, The Great Myth of Urban Britain, BBC, 28 June 2012, http://www.bbc.co.uk/news/uk-18623096 (accessed 31 December 2014).

36. IMF, World Economic Outlook, April 2014. http://www.imf.org/external/Pubs/ft/weo/2014/01/.

37. IMF, World Economic Outlook, April 2014. http://www.imf.org/external/Pubs/ft/weo/2014/01/.

38. Cohort expectation of life at age sixty-five according to historic and projected mortality rates, persons who reached age sixty-five, 1850–2050, 2010-based National Population Projections, ONS, 2012.

39. OBR, Fiscal Sustainability Report, July 2014, p. 8.

40. The Stern Review: The Economics of Climate Change, http://webarchive.nationalarchives.gov.uk/+/http:/www.hm-treasury.gov.uk/media/4/3/executive_summary.pdf (accessed 31 December 2014).

Chapter 1

1. Laura Trevelyan, *A Very British Family: The Trevelyans and their World* (London: I.B.Tauris, 2012), p. 51.

2. Roy Jenkins, *Gladstone* (London: Palgrave Macmillan, 1995), p. 166.

3. Lucy Kellaway, The Ancient Chinese Exam That Inspired Modern Job Recruitment, BBC News, 23 July 2013, http://www.bbc.co.uk/news/magazine-23376561 (accessed 31 December 2014).

4. Ichisada Miyazaki, The Chinese Civil Service Exam System, http://www.gcisd-k12.org/cms/lib4/TX01000829/Centricity/Domain/811/Chinese%20Civil%20Service%20Exam.pdf (accessed 31 December 2014).

5. Peter Gowan, The Origins of the Administrative Elite, *New Left Review* I/162, March–April 1987, http://newleftreview.org/I/162/peter-gowan-the-origins-of-the-administrative-elite (accessed 31 December 2014).

6. Christopher Chantrill, UK Public Spending, http://www.ukpublicspending.co.uk/ (accessed 21 April 2014).

7. History House, How Fast Did News Travel, http://www.historyhouse.co.uk/articles/speed_of_news.html (accessed 31 December 2014).

8. Kate Clements, Podcast 2 Outbreak: 4 August 1914, First World Centenary, http://www.1914.org/podcasts/podcast-2-outbreak-4-august-1914–2/ (accessed 31 December 2014).

9. The TaxPayers' Alliance, *The Single Income Tax: Final Report of the 2020 Tax Commission* (London: The TaxPayers' Alliance, 2012), p. 132.

10. OBR, Economic and Fiscal Outlook, December 2014.

11. IMF, World Economic Outlook, October 2014.

12. Author calculations derived from HM Revenue and Customs, Direct Effects of Illustrative Tax Changes, https://www.gov.uk/government/statistics/direct-effects-of-illustrative-tax-changes (accessed 31 December 2014).

13. Yural Levin, Confirmation Bias and Its Limits, The Corner, *National Review Online*, 9 April 2014, http://www.nationalreview.com/corner/375386/confirmation-bias-and-its-limits-yuval-levin (accessed 31 December 2014).

14. C. Northcote Parkinson, *The Economist*, 10 July 2009, http://www.economist.com/node/13976732 (accessed 31 December 2014).

15. Parkinson's Law, *The Economist*, 19 November 1955, http://www.economist.com/node/14116121 (accessed 31 December 2014).

16. C. M. Turnbull, Parkinson, Cyril Northcote (1909–1993), *Oxford Dictionary of National Biography*, 2007, http://www.oxforddnb.com/view/article/53127 (accessed 31 December 2014).

17. This excludes the Office of the Leader of the House of Commons and the Office of the Leader of the House of Lords (which are part of the Cabinet Office), UK Export Finance (which is part of the Department for Business, Innovation and Skills) and the Office of the Advocate General for Scotland (which, although constitutionally separate, shares offices and its accounts with the Scotland Office).

18. Report of the Machinery of Government Committee, Ministry of Reconstruction, 1918, available at http://www.policy.manchester.ac.uk/media/projects/policymanchester/civilservant/haldanereport.pdf (accessed 31 December 2014).

19. Reorganising central government, National Audit Office, 2010, http://www.nao.org.uk/wp-content/uploads/2010/03/0910452.pdf (accessed 31 December 2014).

20. HM Treasury, Whole of Government Accounts: Year Ended 31 March 2011, October 2012, http://www.hm-treasury.gov.uk/d/whole_of_government_accounts_31-03-2011.pdf (accessed 31 December 2014).

21. Maria Guadalupe, Hongyi Li and Julie Wulf, Who Lives in the C-Suite? Organizational Structure and the Division of Labor in Top Management, Harvard Business School, 2013, http://www.hbs.edu/faculty/Publication%20Files/12–059_040a5ca7-f80c-4d01-abd3–57f431795613.pdf (accessed 31 December 2014).

22. Jamie Merrill, "Worse than Useless": Flood-affected Locals on the Somerset Levels Blame Plight on Environmental Agency, *The Independent*, 4 February 2014, http://www.independent.co.uk/environment/nature/worse-than-useless-floodaffected-locals-on-the-somerset-levels-blame-plight-on-environmental-agency-9107642.html (accessed 31 December 2014).

23. Christopher Booker, Flooding: Somerset Levels Disaster Is Being Driven by EU policy, *The Telegraph*, 8 February 2014, http://www.telegraph.co.uk/comment/columnists/christopherbooker/10625663/Flooding-Somerset-Levels-disaster-is-being-driven-by-EU-policy.html (accessed 31 December 2014).

24. A. Adam, M. D. Delis, and P. Kammas, Fiscal Decentralization and Public Sector Efficiency: Evidence from OECD Countries, CESifo Working Paper No. 2364, 2008.

25. OECD, Fiscal Decentralisation Database – Tax Revenue as Percentage of Total General Government Tax Revenue, http://www.oecd.org/ctp/

federalism/oecdfiscaldecentralisationdatabase.htm#C_Title (accessed 31 December 2014).

26. Grover Noquist et al., *A U-Turn on the Road to Serfdom* (London: Institute of Economic Affairs, 2014).

27. Ryan Bourne and J. R. Shackleton, *The Minimum Wage: Silver Bullet or Poisoned Chalice?* (London: Institute of Economic Affairs, 2014), http://www.iea.org.uk/publications/research/the-minimum-wage-silver-bullet-or-poisoned-chalice (accessed 31 December 2014).

28. Alison Wolf, More Than We Bargained for: The Social and Economic Costs of National Wage Bargaining, CentreForum, 2010, http://www.centreforum.org/assets/pubs/more-than-we-bargained-for.pdf (accessed 31 December 2014).

29. Emma Hall, Carol Propper and John Van Reenen, Can Pay Regulation Kill? Panel Data Evidence on the Effect of Labor Markets on Hospital Performance, Centre for Economic Performance, 2008, http://cep.lse.ac.uk/pubs/download/dp0843.pdf (accessed 31 December 2014).

30. OBR, Historical Office Forecasts Database, November 2013.

31. Decca Aitkenhead, Storm Warning, *The Guardian*, 29 August 2008, http://www.theguardian.com/politics/2008/aug/30/alistairdarling.economy (accessed 31 December 2014).

32. HM Treasury, Forecasts for the UK Economy: A Comparison of Independent Forecasts, March 2008, http://webarchive.nationalarchives.gov.uk/20100407010852/http://www.hm-treasury.gov.uk/d/200803forcomp.pdf (accessed 31 December 2014).

33. Gross Domestic Product Index: CVM: Seasonally adjusted, YBEX, ONS.

34. Philip Coggan, History Lessons for the Markets, the World in 2008, *The Economist*, http://www.economist.com/node/10125401 (accessed 31 December 2014).

35. Minutes of Monetary Policy Committee Meeting, 3 and 4 September 2008, Bank of England, http://www.bankofengland.co.uk/publications/minutes/Documents/mpc/pdf/2008/mpc0809.pdf (accessed 31 December 2014).

36. ONS, CPI All Items: Percentage Change Over 12 Months, D7G7, ONS.

37. OBR, Historical Office Forecasts Database, November 2013.

38. OBR, Public Finances Databank, March 2014.

39. DWP, Benefit Expenditure and Caseload Tables 2014 Table 1a, March 2014.

40. OBR, Public Finances Databank, March 2014.

41. Tim Harford, *The Undercover Economist Strikes Back: How to Run – or Ruin – an Economy* (UK: Hachette, 2013).

42. Valerie A. Ramey, Can Government Purchases Stimulate the Economy?, 2011, http://econweb.ucsd.edu/~vramey/research/JEL_Fiscal_14June2011.pdf (accessed 31 December 2014).

43. Scott Sumner, Why the Fiscal Multiplier Is Roughly Zero, Mercatus Center, 2013, http://mercatus.org/sites/default/files/Sumner_FiscalMultiplier_MOP_090313.pdf (accessed 31 December 2014).

44. Tim Congdon, Why the 1981 Budget Mattered: The End of Naive Keynesianism, in Phillip Booth (ed.), *Were 364 Economists All Wrong?* (London:

Institute of Economic Affairs, 2006), http://www.iea.org.uk/sites/default/files/publications/files/upldbook310pdf.pdf (accessed 31 December 2014).

45. Scott Sumner, Keynesian Confirmation Bias, 30 January 2014, EconL'og, http://econlog.econlib.org/archives/2014/01/keynesian_confi.html (accessed 31 December 2014).

46. J. Bradford Delong, *Budgeting and Macro Policy: A Primer*, Kindle version (U.C. Berkeley, 2012)

47. Paul Krugman, Reckonings; The Japan Syndrome, *New York Times*, 9 February 2000, http://www.nytimes.com/2000/02/09/opinion/reckonings-the-japan-syndrome.html (accessed 31 December 2014).

48. Paul Krugman, Further Notes on Japan's Liquidity Trap, http://www.pkarchive.org/japan/liquid.html (accessed 31 December 2014).

49. Jeffrey Frankel, Over-Optimism in Forecasts by Official Budget Agencies and Its Implications, *Oxford Review of Economic Policy*, 2011.

50. HM Treasury, Budget 2014, https://www.gov.uk/government/uploads/system/uploads/attachment_data/file/293759/37630_Budget_2014_Web_Accessible.pdf, p. 28 (accessed 31 December 2014).

51. Niall Ferguson, *The Cash Nexus*, (New York: Basic Books, 2001), p. 126.

52. Daniel J. Mitchell, How the Swiss 'Debt Brake' Tamed Government, *Wall Street Journal*, 25 April 2012, http://www.wsj.com/articles/SB10001424052702303459004577361622927199902 (accessed 24 February 2015).

53. Katie Allen, National Minimum Wage Not Fit for Purpose, Says Its Founding Father, *The Guardian*, 21 February 2014, http://www.theguardian.com/society/2014/feb/21/national-minimum-wage-not-fit-purpose-sir-george-bain-low-pay (accessed 31 December 2014).

54. Jim Manzi, *Uncontrolled: The Surprising Payoff of Trial-and-Error for Business, Politics, and Society* (New York: Basic Books, 2012).

55. Erik Voeten, Who Predicted Russia's Military Intervention?, The Monkey Cage, 12 March 2014, http://www.washingtonpost.com/blogs/monkey-cage/wp/2014/03/12/who-predicted-russias-military-intervention-2/ (accessed 31 December 2014).

56. Adam Ozimek, The Regulation and Value of Prediction Markets, Mercatus Center, March 2014, http://mercatus.org/sites/default/files/Ozimek_PredictionMarkets_v1.pdf (accessed 31 December 2014).

57. Arrow et al., The Promise of Prediction Markets, *Science*, 2008, http://www.sciencemag.org/content/320/5878/877 (accessed 31 December 2014).

58. Robin Hanson, Shall We Vote on Values, But Bet on Beliefs?, 2007, p. 6, http://hanson.gmu.edu/futarchy.pdf (accessed 31 December 2014).

59. Ozimek, The Regulation and Value of Prediction Markets.

60. Ozimek, The Regulation and Value of Prediction Markets.

Chapter 2

1. The Beatles Tell Us That We've Hit The Concert Price Ceiling, Brian Carpizo, music think tank, 23 December 2010, http://www.musicthinktank.com/blog/the-beatles-tell-us-that-weve-hit-the-concert-price-ceiling.html (accessed 31 December 2014).

2. http://www.tracks.co.uk/acatalog/Rolling_Stones_1963–1964_Concert_Tickets.html (accessed 31 December 2014).

3. Adjusted using RPI.

4. Victoria Ward, Rolling Stones Tickets Remain Unsold after Price Hike, *The Telegraph*, 25 November 2012, http://www.telegraph.co.uk/culture/music/rolling-stones/9701894/Rolling-Stones-tickets-remain-unsold-after-price-hike.html (accessed 31 December 2014).

5. Author calculations derived from Gregory Clark, What Were the British Earnings and Prices Then? (New Series), MeasuringWorth, 2014, http://www.measuringworth.com/ukearncpi/ (accessed 31 December 2014).

6. Lawrence H. Summers, Economic Possibilities for Our Grandchildren, 2013 Martin Feldstein Lecture, p. 5, http://www.nber.org/reporter/2013number4/2013no4.pdf (accessed 31 December 2014).

7. OBR, Fiscal Sustainability Report, July 2014, http://budgetresponsibility.org.uk/pubs/41298-OBR-accessible.pdf (accessed 31 December 2014).

8. ONS, Output per Worker: Whole Economy SA, A4Y, https://www.quandl.com/UKONS/LMS_A4YO_Q-Output-per-Worker-Whole-Economy-change-quarter-on-previous-quarter-SA-UK-Quarterly (accessed 31 December 2014).

9. ONS, Public Sector Productivity Estimates: Total Public Sector, 2010, http://www.ons.gov.uk/ons/rel/psa/public-sector-productivity-estimates--total-public-sector/2010/index.html (accessed 31 December 2014).

10. Andreas Schleicher, You Must Emulate and Innovate to Keep Pace, *TES* magazine, 16 November 2012, http://www.tes.co.uk/article.aspx?storycode=6301764 (accessed 31 December 2014).

11. Christopher Chantrill, UK Public Spending, http://www.ukpublicspending.co.uk/ (accessed 21 April 2014).

12. Lauren Thorpe, Kimberley Trewhitt and James Zuccollo, Must Do Better: Spending on Schools, Reform, May 2013.

13. Graeme Paton, A-Levels "Now Two Grades Easier Than 20 Years Ago", *The Telegraph*, 11 August 2008, http://www.telegraph.co.uk/education/2540628/A-levels-now-two-grades-easier-than-20-years-ago.html (accessed 31 December 2014).

14. Richard Gray, The Body Parts Which Can Be Regrown in a Laboratory, *The Telegraph*, 20 August 2013, http://www.telegraph.co.uk/science/science-news/10275996/The-body-parts-which-can-be-regrown-in-a-laboratory.html (accessed 31 December 2014).

15. John P. A. Ioannidis, Why Most Published Research Findings Are False, 2005, http://www.plosmedicine.org/article/info%3Adoi%2F10.1371%2Fjournal.pmed.0020124 (accessed 31 December 2014).

16. Dominic Cummings, Some Thoughts on Education and Political Priorities, *The Guardian*, http://www.theguardian.com/politics/interactive/2013/oct/11/dominic-cummings-michael-gove-thoughts-education-pdf, p. 63.

17. http://www.youtube.com/user/khanacademy/about (accessed 31 December 2014).

18. Udacity's Sebastian Thrun, Godfather of Free Online Education, Changes Course, Fast Company, 14 November 2013, http://www.fastcompany.com/3021473/udacity-sebastian-thrun-uphill-climb (accessed 31 December 2014).

19. Laura Pappano, The Year of the MOOC, *New York Times*, 2 November 2012, http://www.nytimes.com/2012/11/04/education/edlife/massive-open-online-courses-are-multiplying-at-a-rapid-pace.html (accessed 31 December 2014).

20. Udacity's Sebastian Thrun, Godfather of Free Online Education, Changes Course.

21. William G. Bowen, Matthew M. Chingos, Kelly A. Lack and Thomas I. Nygren, Interactive Learning Online at Public Universities: Evidence from Randomized Trials, May 2012, http://www.sr.ithaka.org/research-publications/interactive-learning-online-public-universities-evidence-randomized-trials (accessed 31 December 2014).

22. Helen Walters, Two Giants of Online Learning Discuss the Future of Education, TED, 28 January 2014, http://blog.ted.com/2014/01/28/in-conversation-salman-khan-sebastian-thrun-talk-online-education/ (accessed 31 December 2014).

23. Arnold Kling, MOOC Spelled Backwards, 3 March 2014, http://www.arnoldkling.com/blog/mooc-spelled-backwards/ (accessed 31 December 2014).

24. Kim Gittleson, Can a Company Live Forever?, BBC, http://www.bbc.co.uk/news/business-16611040

25. Bruce Sterling, Big, Hairy and Agile, Wired, 17 April 2013, http://www.wired.com/beyond_the_beyond/2013/04/big-hairy-and-agile/ (accessed 31 December 2014).

26. Sterling, Big, Hairy and Agile.

27. Rohan Silva, Our IT Future Is Now Hi-Tech, Not High Farce, *The Telegraph*, 10 September 2013, http://www.telegraph.co.uk/technology/10299608/Our-IT-future-is-now-hi-tech-not-high-farce.html (accessed 31 December 2014).

28. Jon Manel, Inside the UK Government Digital Service, BBC, 12 June 2013, http://www.bbc.co.uk/news/uk-politics-22860849 (accessed 31 December 2014).

29. Ben Rooney, U.K. Digital Strategy Receives Praise, *Wall Street Journal*, 12 November 2012, http://blogs.wsj.com/tech-europe/2012/11/12/u-k-digital-strategy-receives-praise/ (accessed 31 December 2014).

30. Jessica Shepherd, Academies to Become a Majority Among State Secondary Schools, *The Guardian*, 5 April 2012, http://www.theguardian.com/education/2012/apr/05/academies-majority-state-secondary-schools (accessed 31 December 2014).

31. Sean Worth, *Better Public Services* (London: Policy Exchange, 2013).

32. Cummings, Some Thoughts on Education and Political Priorities, p. 66.

33. Eric A. Hanushek, The Economic Value of Higher Teacher Quality, 2010, http://www.nber.org/papers/w16606.pdf (accessed 31 December 2014).

34. Ha T. Tue and Jessica H. May, Self-Pay Markets in Health Care: Consumer Nirvana Or Caveat Emptor?, *Health Affairs*, 6 February 2007, http://content.healthaffairs.org/content/suppl/2007/02/09/hlthaff.26.2.w217v1.DC1 (accessed 31 December 2014).

35. Fraser Nelson, Why Tristram Hunt Is Wrong about Free Schools, *The Spectator*, Coffee House, 3 April 2014, http://blogs.spectator.co.uk/coffeehouse/2014/04/why-tristram-hunt-is-wrong-about-free-schools/ (accessed 31 December 2014).

36. Julian Le Grand, *The Other Invisible Hand: Delivering Public Services through Choice and Competition* (Oxford: Princeton University Press, 2007).

37. Paul Graham, How to Be Silicon Valley, 2006, http://paulgraham.com/siliconvalley.html (accessed 31 December 2014).

38. Ryan Lawler, Y Combinator Startups Now Have A Combined Valuation Of $13.7 Billion, Up $2 Billion since June, *TechCrunch*, 25 October 2013, http://techcrunch.com/2013/10/25/y-combinator-13-7b-valuation/ (accessed 31 December 2014).

39. Graham, How to Be Silicon Valley.

40. Philip G. Altbach, The Costs and Benefits of World-Class Universities, 2004, http://bcct.unam.mx/adriana/bibliografia%20parte%202/ALTBACH,%20P.pdf (accessed 31 December 2014).

41. Shailendra Raj Mehta, Why Is Harvard #1? Governance and the Dominance of US Universities, 5 April 2012). http://ssrn.com/abstract=2039675 (accessed 31 December 2014).

42. James Tooley, *Buckingham at 25: Freeing the Universities from State Control* (London: Institute of Economic Affairs, 2001).

43. The annual tuition fee for a doctoral student is around £10,000.

44. Based on total grants of around £487 million per year under new regime funding, and assuming that 4% average annual interest could be gained on an endowment.

Chapter 3

1. Jules Birch, 10 Things You May Not Know about the Beveridge Report, 27 November 2012, http://julesbirch.wordpress.com/2012/11/27/10-things-you-may-not-know-about-the-beveridge-report/ (accessed 31 December 2014).

2. Kristian Niemietz, *A New Understanding of Poverty. Poverty Measurement and Policy Implications*, Research Monograph 65 (London: Institute of Economic Affairs, 2011), pp. 23–26, 56–63.

3. See Liam Byrne's speech to the Social Market Foundation, Renewing the Reward of Responsibility, 23 July 2012.

4. Kristian Niemietz, *Redefining the Poverty Debate. Why a War on Markets Is No Substitute for a War on Poverty*, Research Monograph 67 (London: Institute of Economic Affairs, 2012), pp. 35–41, 146–156.

5. Mike Brewer, How Do Income Support Systems in the UK Affect Labour Force Participation?, Institute for Labour Market Policy Evaluation Working Paper 2009/27, 2009.

6. Child and Working Tax Credit statistics, HM Revenue and Customs, December 2013, p. 8.

7. Institute for Fiscal Studies, Spending by Function, 2014.

8. Niemietz, *Redefining the Poverty Debate*, pp. 43–46.

9. Andrew Hood and Paul Johnson, 70th Anniversary of the Beveridge Report: Where Now for Welfare?, Institute for Fiscal Studies, 2012, http://www.ifs.org.uk/publications/6475 (accessed 31 December 2014).

10. Basil Ernest Vyvyan Sabine, *A History of Income Tax* (London: Routledge, 2005), p. 27.

11. John Jeffrey-Cook, William Pitt and His Taxes, *British Tax Review*, No. 4 (2010), 386.

12. Jeffrey-Cook, William Pitt and His Taxes, p. 387.

13. Income Tax Abolished and Reintroduced, 26 April 2014, http://www.parliament.uk/about/living-heritage/transformingsociety/private-lives/taxation/overview/incometaxbolished/ (accessed 31 December 2014).

14. Author calculations derived from Sally Hills and Thomas Ryland, *The UK Recession in Context – What Do Three Centuries of Data Tell Us? Data Annex* (London: Bank of England, 2010).

15. World War I and a New Approach, a Brief History of Income Tax, HM Revenue & Customs, http://www.hmrc.gov.uk/history/taxhis4.htm (accessed 31 December 2014).

16. Tom Clark and Andrew Dilnot, *Long-term Trends in British Taxation and Spending* (London: Institute for Fiscal Studies, 2002).

17. Clark and Dilnot, *Long-term Trends in British Taxation and Spending.*

18. James Browne and Barra Roantree, *A Survey of the UK Tax System* (London: Institute for Fiscal Studies, 2012), p. 5.

19. Simon Bowers, Abba Admit Outrageous Outfits Were Worn to Avoid Tax, *The Guardian*, 16 February 2014, http://www.theguardian.com/music/2014/feb/16/abba-outfits-tax-deduction-bjorn-ulvaeus (accessed 31 December 2014).

20. The Conference Board, Total Economy Database, January 2014.

21. Edward C. Prescott, Why Do Americans Work So Much More Than Europeans?, NBER Working Paper No. 10316, February 2004.

22. Author calculations derived from Lawrence H. Officer, What Were the UK Earnings and Prices Then?, MeasuringWorth, 2012, http://www.measuringworth.com/ukgdp/ (accessed 31 December 2014).

23. ONS, Annual Survey of Hours and Earnings, 2013 Provisional Results.

24. Niemetz, *Redefining the Poverty Debate*, pp. 209–217.

25. Branko Milanovic, Global Income Inequality by the Numbers: In History and Now, The World Bank, 2012, http://elibrary.worldbank.org/doi/pdf/10.1596/1813-9450-6259 (accessed 31 December 2014).

26. Bill & Melinda Gates, 2014 Gates Annual Letter, http://annualletter.gatesfoundation.org/ accessed 31 December 2014)

27. João Paulo Pessoa and John Van Reenen, Decoupling of Wage Growth and Productivity Growth? Myth and Reality, Centre for Economic Performance, 2013, http://cep.lse.ac.uk/pubs/download/dp1246.pdf (accessed 31 December 2014).

28. Stephen Ansolabehere, John M. de Figueiredo and James M. Snyder, Jr., Are Campaign Contributions Investment in the Political Marketplace or Individual Consumption? Or Why Is There So Little Money in Politics?, 2002, http://web.mit.edu/jdefig/www/papers/invest_or_consumpt.pdf (accessed 31 December 2014).

29. Daniel W. Sacks, Betsey Stevenson and Justin Wolfers, The New Stylized Facts about Income and Subjective Well-Being, CESifo Working Paper No. 4067, January 2013.

30. Will Wilkinson, In Pursuit of Happiness Research Is It Reliable? What Does It Imply for Policy?, Cato Institute, 2007, http://www.cato.org/sites/cato.org/files/pubs/pdf/pa590.pdf (accessed 31 December 2014).

31. William D. Nordhaus, Schumpeterian Profits in the American Economy: Theory and Measurement, 2004, http://www.nber.org/papers/w10433 (accessed 31 December 2014).

32. Stephen Burgen, Spain Youth Unemployment Reaches Record 56.1%, *The Guardian*, 20 August 2013, http://www.theguardian.com/business/2013/aug/30/spain-youth-unemployment-record-high (accessed 31 December 2014).

33. Megan McArdle, *The Up Side of Down: Why Failing Well Is the Key to Success* (New York: Penguin, 2014), Kindle location 2616.

34. Erik Brynjolfsson and Andrew McAfee, *Race Against The Machine: How the Digital Revolution Is Accelerating Innovation, Driving Productivity, and Irreversibly Transforming Employment and the Economy* (Lexington, MA: Digital Frontier Press, 2011).

35. James W. Vaupel and Kristín G. v. Kistowski, Broken Limits to Life Expectancy, Max Planck Institute for Demographic Research, 2005 http://www.ageing.ox.ac.uk/files/AH%203%20Vaupel%20and%20v_Kistowski.pdf (accessed 31 December 2014).

36. ONS, National Population Projections, 2010-Based Projections, 2011.

37. Matt Ridley, Why Are There So Few People Over 115 Years of Age?, 2013, http://www.rationaloptimist.com/blog/why-are-there-so-few-people-over-115-years-of-age.aspx (accessed 31 December 2014).

38. Allister Heath, People Too Scared to Save Because They Don't Trust Politicians, *City A.M.*, 6 March 2014, http://www.cityam.com/article/1394071048/people-too-scared-save-because-they-don-t-trust-politicians (accessed 31 December 2014).

39. Philip Booth and Kristian Niemietz, Pension Privatisation by Choice, in Thom Reilly (ed.), *Pensions: Policies, New Reforms and Current Challenges* (New York: Nova Publishers, 2014).

40. Gabriel Heller Sahlgren, Income from work – the Fourth Pillar of Income Provision in Old Age, Institute of Economic Affairs, 2014, http://www.iea.org.uk/sites/default/files/publications/files/Income%20from%20work%20web.pdf (accessed 31 December 2014).

41. Gabriel Heller Sahlgren, Work Longer, Live Healthier, Institute of Economic Affairs, 2013, http://www.iea.org.uk/sites/default/files/publications/files/Work%20Longer,%20Live_Healthier.pdf (accessed 31 December 2014).

42. S. A. Mathieson, How Andrew Dilnot and Social Care Might Save the NHS, *The Guardian*, 26 October 2011, http://www.guardian.co.uk/healthcare-network/2011/oct/26/andrew-dilnot-social-care-save-nhs (accessed 31 December 2014).

43. Richard Humphries, Social Care Funding and the NHS Crisis, Kings Fund, 2011, http://www.kingsfund.org.uk/sites/files/kf/social-care-funding-nhs-crisis-kings-fund-march-2011.pdf, p. 10 (accessed 31 December 2014).

44. Joyce Francis, An Overview of the UK Domiciliary Care Sector, UKHCA Summary Paper, United Kingdom Homecare Association, February 2013,

http://www.ukhca.co.uk/pdfs/domiciliarycaresectoroverview.pdf, p. 6 (accessed 31 December 2014).

45. Melanie Arntz, Ralf Sacchetto, Alexander Spermann, Susanne Steffes, and Sarah Widmaier, The German Social Long-Term Care Insurance: Structure and Reform Options, Institute for the Study of Labor, 2007, http://ftp.iza.org/dp2625.pdf, p. 11 (accessed 31 December 2014).

46. Caroline Glendinning and Nicola Moran, Reforming Long Term Care: Recent Lessons from Other Countries, Social Policy Research Unit, University of York, June 2009, http://www.york.ac.uk/inst/spru/research/pdf/LTCare.pdf (accessed 31 December 2014).

47. Francis, An Overview of the UK Domiciliary Care Sector, p. 8.

Chapter 4

1. Conference Board, Total Economy Database GDP per Person Employed in 2014 EKS$, January 2014, https://www.conference-board.org/data/economydatabase/ (accessed 31 December 2014).

2. Nicholas Crafts, The Industrial Revolution: Economic Growth in Britain, 1700–1860, *ReFRESH*, Spring, 1987, http://www.ehs.org.uk/dot Asset/15457c19-e7bd-4045-a056-30a3efac2d47.pdf (accessed 31 December 2014).

3. ONS, 170 Years of Industrial Change across England and Wales, 5 June 2013, http://www.ons.gov.uk/ons/rel/census/2011-census-analysis/170-years-of-industry/170-years-of-industrial-changeponent.html (accessed 31 December 2014).

4. Historical Timeline – Farmers & the Land, Growing a Nation – the Story of American Agriculture, http://www.agclassroom.org/gan/timeline/farmers_land.htm (accessed 31 December 2014).

5. ONS, 170 Years of Industrial Change across England and Wales, 5 June 2013, http://www.ons.gov.uk/ons/rel/census/2011-census-analysis/170-years-of-industry/170-years-of-industrial-changeponent.html

6. Stephen Broadberry and Tim Leunig, *The Impact of Government Policies on UK Manufacturing since 1945* (London: Foresight, Government Office for Science, Department for Business, Innovation and Skills, 2013), p. 4.

7. Henry Foy, UK's Resurgent Car Industry Still Faces Challenges, *Financial Times*, 7 January 2014, http://www.ft.com/cms/s/0/b096187e-7784-11e3-807e-00144feabdc0.html#axzz2ws7CKvVv (accessed 31 December 2014).

8. UK Car Exports Hit Record Despite European Market Slump, 17 January 2013, http://www.bbc.co.uk/news/business-21057798 (accessed 31 December 2014).

9. Emma Rowley, First Trade Surplus in Cars since 1976, *The Telegraph*, 15 May 2012, http://www.telegraph.co.uk/finance/economics/9267231/First-trade-surplus-in-cars-since-1976.html (accessed 31 December 2014).

10. Jonathan Haskel and Stian Westlake, Look to the Intangibles, *The Economist*, 20 February 2014, http://www.economist.com/blogs/freeexchange/2014/02/investment?fsrc=scn%2Ftw_ec%2Flook_to_the_intangibles (accessed 31 December 2014).

11. Peter Goodridge, Jonathan Haskel and Gavin Wallis, Can Intangible Investment Explain the UK Productivity Puzzle?, *National Institute Economic Review*, 2013, http://ner.sagepub.com/content/224/1/R48. short?rss=1&ssource=mfr (accessed 31 December 2014).

12. Open Skies and Flights of Fancy, *The Economist*, 2 October 2003, http://www.economist.com/node/2099875 (accessed 31 December 2014).

13. Robert W. Poole Jr. and Viggo Butler, *Airline Deregulation: The Unfinished Revolution*, RPPI, 1998, http://cei.org/pdf/1451.pdf (accessed 31 December 2014).

14. Fred L. Smith Jr. and Braden Cox, Airline Deregulation, *Concise Encyclopaedia of Economics*, 2008, http://www.econlib.org/library/Enc/AirlineDeregulation.html (accessed 31 December 2014).

15. Open Skies and Flights of Fancy.

16. Smith and Cox, Airline Deregulation.

17. Elizabeth E. Bailey, Airline Deregulation – Confronting the Paradoxes, *Cato Review of Business & Government*, 1992, http://object.cato.org/sites/cato.org/files/serials/files/regulation/1992/7/v15n3-3.pdf (accessed 31 December 2014).

18. Matt Ridley, *The Rational Optimist* (New York: HarperCollins, 2010), p. 113.

19. Ryan Bourne, What Did Privatisation Do for Us?, Centre for Policy Studies, 2013, http://www.cps.org.uk/blog/q/date/2013/04/16/what-did-privatisation-do-for-us/ (accessed 31 December 2014).

20. Tony Lodge, Rail's Second Chance, Centre for Policy Studies, 2013, http://www.cps.org.uk/files/reports/original/130321100013-railssecondchance.pdf (accessed 31 December 2014).

21. Growth and Prosperity – How Franchising helped Transform the Railway into a British Success Story, Association of Train Operating Companies, 2013, http://www.atoc.org/download/clientfiles/files/Growth%20and%20Prosperity%20Report.pdf (accessed 31 December 2014).

22. Realising the Potential of GB Rail – Report of the Rail Value for Money Study, 2011.

23. Lodge, Rail's Second Chance.

24. Coming Round the Bend, *The Economist*, 20 June 2013, http://www.economist.com/news/britain/21579836-how-britain-developed-truly-competitive-rail-freight-market-coming-round-bend (accessed 31 December 2014).

25. Lodge, Rail's Second Chance, p. 36

26. As reported by the House of Commons Treasury Select Committee report, *Competition and Choice in Retail Banking*, 2011. On customer service ratings, a survey of 13,000 people by *Which?* in 2011 found none of the large banks scored highly. First Direct, The Co-operative Bank, The One Account, Smile and Yorkshire Building Society topped the ratings.

27. *Which?*, September 2012.

28. Reported in the *Financial Times*, 25 October 2012.

29. Reported in the *Financial Times*, 25 October 2012.

30. Evidence variously submitted to the Treasury Select Committee, as part of the Independent Commission on Banking, which reported 18 October 2011.

31. Reported in the *Financial Times*, 5 July 2012.

32. The BBC Takes to the Airwaves (14 November 1922) http://News.Bbc. Co.Uk/Aboutbbcnews/Spl/Hi/History/Noflash/Html/1920s.Stm (accessed 31 December 2014).

33. Tim Montgomerie, The BBC Has a Monopoly and It's Abusing It, ConservativeHome, 11 July 2011, http://www.conservativehome.com/platform/2011/07/the-bbc-has-a-monopoly-and-its-abusing-it-says-timmontgomerie.html (accessed 31 December 2014).

34. The Communications Market, UK, Ofcom, 2010, http://www.ofcom.org.uk/static/cmr-10/UKCM-3.17.html (accessed 31 December 2014).

35. Paul Krugman, Why Most Economists' Predictions Are Wrong, *The Red Herring* http://web.archive.org/web/19980610100009/www.redherring. com/mag/issue55/economics.html (accessed 31 December 2014).

36. Tyler Cowen, *Average Is Over* (New York: Penguin, 2013), p. 43.

37. Daniel B. Klein and Alexander Tabarrok, Is the FDA Safe and Effective?, http://www.fdareview.org/ (accessed 31 December 2014).

38. Brady Dennis, FDA Review of New Sunscreen Ingredients Has Languished for Years, Frustrating Advocates, *Washington Post*, 20 March 2014, http://www.washingtonpost.com/national/health-science/fda-review-of-new-sunscreen-ingredients-languishes-frustrating-advocates/2014/03/20/be85a288-a9fc-11e3-9e82-8064fcd31b5b_story.html (accessed 31 December 2014).

39. Adam Theier, Permissionless Innovation, Mercatus Center, 2014 http://mercatus.org/sites/default/files/Permissionless.Innovation.web__0.pdf (accessed 31 December 2014).

40. ONS, Business Demography, 2011, http://www.ons.gov.uk/ons/rel/busregister/business-demography/2011/stb-business-demography-2011.html#tab-Business-survivals (accessed 31 December 2014).

41. http://www.heritage.org/index/visualize?countries=unitedstates&type=10 (accessed 31 December 2014).

42. http://www.heritage.org/index/visualize?countries=unitedkingdom&type=10 (accessed 31 December 2014).

43. CBI, Thinking Positive: The 21st Century Employment Relationship, 2011, http://content.yudu.com/A1sg86/CBI-Thinkingpositive/resources/index.htm?referrerUrl=, p. 10 (accessed 6 November 2012).

44. Institute of Directors, *Regulation Reckoner. Counting the Real Cost of Regulation* (London: IOD, 2011), p. 1.

45. Open Europe, *Repatriation of EU Social Policy: The Right Focus for a Conservative Government* (November 2009), p. 7.

Chapter 5

1. House of Commons Energy and Climate Change Committee, Energy Prices, Profits and Poverty, Energy and Climate Change Select Committee, 16 July 2013, http://www.publications.parliament.uk/pa/cm201314/cmselect/cmenergy/108/10806.htm (accessed 31 December 2014).

2. Emily Gosden and Rowena Mason, Risk of UK Blackouts Has Tripled in a Year, Ofgem Warns, *The Telegraph*, 27 June 2013, http://www.telegraph.co.uk/finance/newsbysector/energy/10145803/Risk-of-UK-blackouts-has-tripled-in-a-year-Ofgem-warns.html (accessed 31 December 2014).

3. Intergovernmental Panel on Climate Change, Climate Change 2013: The Physical Science Basis – IPCC Working Group I Contribution to AR5, http://www.climatechange2013.org/images/report/WG1AR5_Chapter10_FINAL.pdf (accessed 31 December 2014).

4. Committee on Climate Change, Setting a Target for Emission Reduction, http://www.theccc.org.uk/tackling-climate-change/the-science-of-climate-change/setting-a-target-for-emission-reduction/ (accessed 31 December 2014).

5. Jennifer Webber, CO_2 emissions 2013 Q4, The Department of Energy and Climate Change (DECC), Press release, March 27, 2014.

6. Dieter Helm, *The Carbon Crunch: How We're Getting Climate Change Wrong – and How to Fix It* (New Haven, CT: Yale University Press, 2012), p. 94.

7. Warren Hatter, Government Should Be Open about 'Outsourced Emissions' According to Committee, Energy and Climate Change Committee, 18 April 2012, http://www.parliament.uk/business/committees/committees-a-z/commons-select/energy-and-climate-change-committee/news/consumption-published/ (accessed 31 December 2014).

8. Andrew Leonard, Jimmy Carter – the Peak Oil President, *Salon*, 6 August 2008, http://www.salon.com/2008/08/06/jimmy_carter_peak_oil/ (accessed 31 December 2014).

9. Helm, *The Carbon Crunch*, 2012, p. 141.

10. Leonardo Maugeri, The Unprecedented Upsurge of Oil Production Capacity and What It Means for the World, Harvard Kennedy School Belfer Center for Science and International Affairs, 25 June 2012, http://belfercenter.ksg.harvard.edu/files/Presentation%20on%20Oil-%20The%20Next%20Revolution.pdf (accessed 31 December 2014).

11. Zhongmin Wang and Alan Krupnick, A Retrospective Review of Shale Gas Development in the United States, Resources for the Future, April 2013, http://www.rff.org/RFF/documents/RFF-DP-13-12.pdf (accessed 31 December 2014).

12. Helm, *The Carbon Crunch*, 2012, p. 143.

13. Matt Ridley, Let's Get Fracking, and Slash Our Gas Bills, *The Telegraph*, 4 December 2012, http://www.telegraph.co.uk/earth/energy/9721493/Lets-get-fracking-and-slash-our-gas-bills.html (accessed 31 December 2014).

14. Matt Ridley, The Shale Gas Shock, Global Warming Policy Foundation, 2011, http://www.marcellus.psu.edu/resources/PDFs/shalegas_GWPF.pdf (accessed 31 December 2014).

15. This is also, of course, partially down to the recession.

16. Parliamentary Office of Science and Technology, UK Shale Gas Potential, July 2013, http://www.parliament.uk/documents/post/ShaleGas_POSTbox.pdf (accessed 31 December 2014).

17. Corin Taylor, Getting Shale Gas Working, Institute of Directors (IoD) Report, 2013.

18. Daniel Yergin, *The Prize: The Epic Quest for Oil, Money & Power* (New York: Free Press, 2008), p. 651.

19. Matt Ridley, The Dash for Shale Oil Will Shake the World, 6 July 2013, http://www.rationaloptimist.com/blog/the-dash-for-shale-oil-will-shake-the-world.aspx (accessed 31 December 2014).

20. The Future of Oil: Yesterday's Fuel. *The Economist*, 3 August 2013, http://www.economist.com/news/leaders/21582516-worlds-thirst-oil-could-be-nearing-peak-bad-news-producers-excellent (accessed 31 December 2014).

21. Assuming the average kettle uses 2,500 W.

22. Author calculation derived from David J. C. MacKay, *Sustainable Energy – Without the Hot Air* (Cambridge: UIT, 2008) and a UK land area of 243,610 km^2 and producing 120 GW.

23. Author calculation derived from MacKay, *Sustainable Energy*, using 3 W/m^2 for power generated and a shallow water size of 40,000 km^2.

24. Ramez Naam, Smaller, Cheaper, Faster: Does Moore's Law Apply to Solar Cells?, 16 March 2011, http://blogs.scientificamerican.com/guest-blog/2011/03/16/smaller-cheaper-faster-does-moores-law-apply-to-solar-cells/ (accessed 31 December 2014).

25. Schalk Cloete, The Fundamental Limitations of Renewable Energy, *The Energy Collective*, 6 August 2013, http://theenergycollective.com/schalk-cloete/257351/fundamental-limitations-renewable-energy (accessed 31 December 2014).

26. Author calculation derived from MacKay, *Sustainable Energy*, and a UK land area of 243,610 km^2 and producing 120 GW.

27. Mark Easton, The Great Myth of Urban Britain, BBC, 28 June 2013, http://www.bbc.co.uk/news/uk-18623096 (accessed 31 December 2014).

28. MacKay, *Sustainable Energy*, http://www.withouthotair.com/c25/page_178.shtml (accessed 31 December 2014).

29. Dieter Helm, *Energy, the State, and the Market: British Energy Policy since 1979* (Oxford: Oxford University Press, 2003).

30. Helm, *Energy, the State and the Market*, p. 27.

31. Paul Bolton, Energy Prices, House of Commons Library, 31 January 2014, http://www.parliament.uk/business/publications/research/briefing-papers/SN04153/energy-prices (accessed 31 December 2014).

32. Emily Gosden, Coal's Final Chapter Is Not yet Written, *The Telegraph*, 31 March 2013, http://www.telegraph.co.uk/finance/newsbysector/energy/9963385/Coals-final-chapter-is-not-yet-written.html (accessed 31 December 2014).

33. Department of Energy & Climate Change, Planning Our Electric Future: A White Paper for Secure, Affordable and Low-Carbon Electricity, Policy Paper, DECC, 12 July 2011, https://www.gov.uk/government/uploads/system/uploads/attachment_data/file/48129/2176-emr-white-paper.pdf (accessed 31 December 2014).

34. Energy and Climate Change Select Committee, Building New Nuclear: The Challenges Ahead, 2013, http://www.publications.parliament.uk/pa/cm201213/cmselect/cmenergy/117/11703.htm (accessed 31 December 2014).

35. David Jolly, Finnish Nuclear Plant Won't Open until 2016, *New York Times*, 11 February 2013, http://www.nytimes.com/2013/02/12/business/global/ finnish-nuclear-plant-wont-open-until-2016.html (accessed 31 December 2014).

36. BBC, Finland's Olkiluoto 3 Nuclear Plant Delayed Again, *News Europe*, 16 July 2012, http://www.bbc.co.uk/news/world-europe-18862422 (accessed 31 December 2014).

37. Richard Tol, Bogus Prophecies of Doom Will Not Fix the Climate, *Financial Times*, 31 March 2014.

Chapter 6

1. First new port in the UK for more than 20 years opens this week, Mark Odell, *Financial Times*, 3 November 2013, http://www.ft.com/cms/s/0/63ba9114-431e-11e3-9d3c-00144feabdc0.html#axzz2xM5Ykl21 (accessed 31 December 2014).

2. Dockers' Return, *The Economist*, 8 December 2011, http://www.economist.com/node/21541456 (accessed 31 December 2014).

3. Alistair Osborne, Britain Makes Way for New £1.5bn Superport, *The Telegraph*, 26 May 2012, http://www.telegraph.co.uk/finance/newsbysector/transport/9291583/Britain-makes-way-for-new-1.5bn-superport.html (accessed 31 December 2014).

4. Giants of the Sea Help Drive UK Port Expansion, *Financial Times*, 16 June 2013.

5. Department for Transport, *National Policy Statement for Ports* (London: Stationery Office, 2012), pp. 13–14.

6. ONS series BOKI (Balance of Payments, Goods), ENXQ (Balance of Payments, Oil).

7. IMF, World Economic Outlook, October 2014.

8. Jemima Kiss, ABCes: Mail Online Presses Ahead as Rivals See Post-World Cup Dip, *The Guardian*, 26 August 2010, http://www.guardian.co.uk/media/2010/aug/26/abces-july-2010 (accessed 31 December 2014).

9. Edward Glaesar, *The Triumph of the City: How Our Greatest Invention Makes Us Richer, Smarter, Greener, Healthier, and Happier* (New York: Penguin, 2011), p. 1.

10. John D. Kasarda and Grey Lindsay, *Aerotropolis: The Way We'll Live Next* (New York: Farrar, Straus and Giroux, 2011).

11. Glaesar, *The Triumph of the City*.

12. Edward Glaesar, A Happy Tale of Two Cities, *New York Daily News*, 13 October 2013, http://www.nydailynews.com/opinion/happy-tale-cities-article-1.1483174 (accessed 31 December 2014).

13. Cabinet Office, Tech City Celebrates Third Anniversary as New Figures Show Economic Success Story, 2013, https://www.gov.uk/government/news/tech-city-celebrates-third-anniversary-as-new-figures-show-economic-success-story (accessed 31 December 2014).

14. Sally Davies, DeepMind and NaturalMotion Lead Charge of London's Tech Start-Ups, *Financial Times*, 10 February 2014, http://www.ft.com/cms/s/0/484ade12-9278-11e3-8018-00144feab7de.html#slide0 (accessed 31 December 2014).

15. John O'Ceallaigh, London Named the Most Popular City in the World, *The Telegraph*, 17 January 2014, http://www.telegraph.co.uk/travel/destinations/europe/uk/london/10579211/London-named-the-most-popular-city-in-the-world.html (accessed 31 December 2014).

16. Neil O'Brien, Another Country, *The Spectator*, 14 April 2012.

17. Emma Duncan, On a High, *The Economist*, 30 June 2012.

18. Wikipedia, Global City, http://en.wikipedia.org/wiki/Global_city (accessed 31 December 2014).

19. Daniel Knowles, 13 Charts That Show Why London Is Basically Another Country, *Buzzfeed*, 17 March 2014, http://www.buzzfeed.com/dlknowles/14-reasons-why-london-should-be-independent-and-o-fm44 (accessed 31 December 2014).

20. Glaesar, *The Triumph of the City*.

21. Stop Project Pinewood, http://www.stopprojectpinewood.webeden.co.uk/ (accessed 31 December 2014).

22. Pinewood Studio Plans Rejected by South Bucks Council, 15 May 2013, http://www.bbc.co.uk/news/uk-england-beds-bucks-herts-22537468 (accessed 31 December 2014).

23. Alex Morton, *Cities for Growth* (London: Policy Exchange, 2011).

24. Daniel Knowles, 15 facts that Reveal the Utter Insanity of Britain's Housing Market, *Buzzfeed*, 29 October 2012, http://www.buzzfeed.com/dlknowles/britains-dysfunctional-property-market-in-gi-fm44 (accessed 31 December 2014).

25. Kristian Niemietz, *Redefining the Poverty Debate: Why a War on Markets Is No Substitute for a War on Poverty* (London: Institute of Economic Affairs, 2012).

26. DWP, Expenditure by Benefit, £ Million, Real Terms (2014/15 prices), April 2014.

27. Niemietz, *Redefining the Poverty Debate*.

28. Alex Morton, *Taxing Issues? Reducing Housing Demand or Increasing Housing Supply* (London: Policy Exchange, 2013).

29. Alex Morton, *Why Aren't We Building Enough Attractive Homes?* (London: Policy Exchange, 2012).

30. Morton, *Why Aren't We Building Enough Attractive Homes?*

31. Morton, *Cities for Growth*.

32. Tim Leunig, Community Land Auctions, CentreForum, 2011.

33. Richard Dobbs, Jaana Remes, James Manyika, Charles Roxburgh, Sven Smit and Fabian Schaer, Urban World: Cities and the Rise of the Consuming Class (McKinsey Global Institute, 2012), http://www.mckinsey.com/insights/urbanization/urban_world_cities_and_the_rise_of_the_consuming_class (accessed 31 December 2014).

34. Reuters, The Swelling Middle, 2012, http://www.reuters.com/middle-class-infographic (accessed 31 December 2014).

35. Open Europe, Repatriating EU Social Policy: The Best Choice for Jobs and Growth?, 7 November 2011.

36. Andrew Trotman, Iceland First European Country to Sign Free Trade Agreement with China, *The Telegraph*, 15 April 2013, http://www.telegraph.co.uk/finance/economics/9995525/Iceland-first-European-country-to-sign-free-trade-agreement-with-China.html (accessed 31 December 2014).

37. Louise Armistead, Future of UK Exports Is with BRICS Not Europe, Says O'Neill, *The Telegraph*, 5 March 2013, http://www.telegraph.co.uk/finance/financialcrisis/9911119/Future-of-UK-exports-is-with-Brics-not-Europe-says-ONeill.html (accessed 31 December 2014).

38. Philip Aldrick, UK Doubles Exports to BRICS Since Crisis, *The Telegraph*, 18 February 2013, http://www.telegraph.co.uk/finance/economics/9876267/UK-doubles-exports-to-BRICS-since-crisis.html (accessed 31 December 2014).

39. Nicholas Cecil, Heathrow Airport Expansion "Ruled Out for 10 Years" by Aviation Minister, *Evening Standard*, 19 April 2012, http://www.thisislondon.co.uk/news/transport/heathrow-airport-expansion-ruled-out-for-10-years-by-aviation-minister-7660858.html (accessed 31 December 2014).

40. Greater London Authority, *A New Airport for London* (London: Greater London Authority, 2011).

41. Oonagh Shiel, Research Confirms Connectivity Crunch Costing UK Economy, Cheapflights.co.uk, 27 January 2012, http://news.cheapflights.co.uk/research-confirms-connectivity-crunch-costing-uk-economy/ (accessed 31 December 2014).

42. British Chambers of Commerce, *The Economic Impact of Hub Airports*, (London: British Chambers of Commerce, 2009).

43. Greater London Authority, *A New Airport for London*.

44. Keith Boyfield, *Plane Commonsense: The Case for Feeder-Reliever Airports in the South East* (London: Adam Smith Institute, 1994).

45. British Chambers of Commerce, *The Economic Impact of Hub Airports*

46. Paul Maynard, *UK Aviation Industry on the Precipice*, 2011.

47. Frontier Economics, *Connecting for Growth: The Role of Britain's Hub Airport in Economic Recovery*, 2011.

48. Maynard, *UK Aviation Industry on the Precipice*.

49. Kasarda and Lindsay, *Aerotropolis: The Way We'll Live Next*.

50. Malcolm Moore, China to Build World's Biggest Airport, *The Telegraph*, 9 September 2011, http://www.telegraph.co.uk/news/worldnews/asia/china/8752665/China-to-build-worlds-biggest-airport.html (accessed 31 December 2014).

51. Voltaire, On the Church of England, http://chnm.gmu.edu/revolution/d/272/ (accessed 31 December 2014).

52. Harry Cockburn, "Hyper-Productive" Immigrant Entrepreneurs Have Founded 1 in 7 UK Firms, *London Loves Business*, 5 March 2014, http://www.londonlovesbusiness.com/business-news/politics/hyper-productive-immigrant-entrepreneurs-have-founded-1-in-7-uk-firms/7602.article (accessed 31 December 2014).

53. Ryan Bourne, Work: Have Immigrants "Taken Our Jobs"?, *ConservativeHome*, 1 November 2013, http://www.conservativehome.com/platform/2013/11/work-have-immigrants-taken-our-jobs.html (accessed 31 December 2014).

54. The History of a "City without History", *Asia Society*, 2010, http://asiasociety.org/business/development/history-city-without-history (accessed 31 December 2014).

55. The Boomerang Effect, *The Economist*, 19 April 2012, http://www.economist.com/node/21552898 (accessed 31 December 2014).

56. http://shenzhen.made-in-china.com/info/about-shenzhen.html (accessed 31 December 2014).

57. The End of Cheap China, *The Economist*, 8 March 2012, http://www.economist.com/node/21549956 (accessed 31 December 2014).

58. The More Special Economic Zone, *The Economist*, 5 July 2012, http://www.economist.com/node/21558307 (accessed 31 December 2014).

59. Sebastian Mallaby, The Politically Incorrect Guide to Ending Poverty, *The Atlantic*, 8 June 2010, http://www.theatlantic.com/magazine/archive/2010/07/the-politically-incorrect-guide-to-ending-poverty/308134/?single_page=true (accessed 31 December 2014).

60. IMF, World Economic Outlook, 2012.

61. World Bank, *Special Economic Zones: Performance, Lessons Learned, and Implications for Zone Development* (Washington DC, World Bank, 2008).

62. http://www.oecd.org/mena/49226268.pdf (accessed 31 December 2014).

63. http://www.oecd.org/mena/investment/41613492.pdf (accessed 31 December 2014).

64. Don Hirasuna and Joel Michael, Enterprise Zones: A Review of the Economic Theory and Empirical Evidence, Minnesota House of Representatives Research Department, 2005, http://www.house.leg.state.mn.us/hrd/pubs/entzones.pdf (accessed 31 December 2014).

65. OECD, *Tax Policy Reform and Economic Growth*, OECD Tax Policy Studies, No. 20 (Paris: OECD Publishing, 2010), p. 3.

66. OECD, *Tax Policy Reform and Economic Growth*, p. 50.

67. Institute for Fiscal Studies, *Tax by Design*, Mirrlees Review, 2012, p. 418.

68. http://www.kpmg.com/Global/en/IssuesAndInsights/ArticlesPublications/Documents/corporate-and-indirect-tax-rate-survey-2011.pdf (accessed 31 December 2014).

69. Institute for Fiscal Studies, *Tax by Design*.

THE FREE ENTERPRISE MANIFESTO

GOVERNMENT:

We should cut down central government, and focus it on what it can do best:

1) We should streamline the government, outsourcing administration, and halving the number of government departments.
2) We should regionalise the national minimum wage, abolish national pay bargaining and examine the case for significant fiscal decentralisation.
3) We should stop trying to control the business cycle with the budget deficit. Instead, we should adopt an automatic debt brake-balanced budget rule.
4) We should stop relying so heavily on fundamentally uncertain official forecasts. We should create new prediction markets to forecast GDP and unemployment.

PUBLIC SERVICES:

We should use choice, experimentation and profit to drive genuine innovation:

5) We should introduce new legal rights for individual choice in public services and a purchaser–provider split in every area of the public sector where this is practical.
6) We should allow free schools to generate a profit to encourage the development of new academy chains. Public bodies should be encouraged to earn extra revenue by selling their services abroad.
7) We should set universities free by giving them more autonomy over their funding, access, bursaries and research agenda.

TAXATION AND WELFARE:

We should increase the rewards for work and saving:

8) We should automatically increase tax thresholds with the higher of inflation or average earnings.
9) We should convert Jobseekers' Allowance into a repayable loan for those under twenty-five without a long record of national insurance contributions. Those over twenty-five should get more time to find work, depending on their record.
10) We should replace maternity and paternity pay with a flat Baby Bonus paid out directly by the government.
11) We should create Care ISAs, a new tax-free investment vehicle to encourage us all to save more for our own social care. Individuals should be given the choice of taking a cash payment for their social care.

INDUSTRIAL POLICY:

We should reduce the barriers to entry and increase competition to drive improvements in productivity:

12) We should introduce a range of measures to increase competition across UK industries:
    a. Full account portability in the banking system.
    b. Separating Network Rail into regional franchises.
    c. Converting the BBC licence fee into a voluntary subscription.
13) We should reform bankruptcy law to give individual entrepreneurs more protection.
14) We should allow the first ten employees to be registered as self-employed.

ENERGY:

We should rely on markets rather than government to plan the industry's future:

15) We should minimise the barriers to the development of a UK shale gas industry.

16) We should gradually phase out the current system of subsidies for renewable energy.

17) We should increase subsidies and introduce prizes for advances in basic research.

18) We should cut current taxes on carbon to a level consistent with international best estimates of its social cost. As we gain more evidence, we can look to whether these taxes should be further lowered or steadily raised.

TRADE:

We should turn Britain into a world crossroads for trade, innovation and investment:

19) We should seek to retain London's position as a world leader by making it easier for private developers to build new housing and aviation capacity.

20) We should introduce a new system of market-based immigration visas.

21) We should seek to renegotiate EU treaties in order to reduce the burden of labour regulation, among other things.

22) We should lower the headline rate of corporation tax to 10% and phase out other damaging business taxes.

Index

1945 election, 3–5

ageing population, 15, 77–78
automation, 14, 75–76
aviation, 98–100, 141–143

banking, 103–105, 108
Baumol cost disease, 42–44
BBC, 105–107
Beveridge Report, 5, 60–65

cities, 133
climate change, 15, 112–115,
    127–128
competition, 6, 9–10, 52–54, 94–95,
    98–107
contributory principle, 70–71
corporate taxes, 148–149

devolution, 28–31
disruption, 11–12, 49–50, 107–109

education, 44–46, 51–53
emergent order, 9–12
energy market, 113, 122–126
Enterprise Zones, 146–147
ethics, 8–9, 13–14, 52

financial crisis, 2, 7–8, 32
fiscal rules, 32, 37
forecasting, 32, 35–40

globalisation, 15, 132, 139–141
Government Digital Service (GDS),
    50–51
Great Depression, 1, 5–6

health, 45–46, 51
housing, 136–138

immigration, 144–145
income tax, 65–69

industrial policy, 13, 94–95, 121
Industrial Revolution, 12, 93
inequality, 72–75

Keynesianism, 5, 6, 33–35, 38

living standards, 12, 43, 74
London, 129, 133–136

Machinery of Government, 26–28
manufacturing, 93–96
MOOCs, 47–49

nationalisation, 4, 94–95
Northcote-Trevelyan report, 21–22

Parkinson's Law, 25
peak oil, 115–117
pensions, 78–83
planning, 15, 135–138
prediction markets, 39–41
privatisation, 98–102
prizes, 121–122
productivity, 91–93, 97–98
public sector productivity, 43–44, 53

railways, 102–103
regulation, 108–111
renewable energy, 119–121

savings, 82–83, 131–132
shale gas, 117–119
Silver, Nate, 37–41
size of the state, 1, 22–24, 43–44
social care, 83–87

tax credits, 64, 67–68
Thrun, Sebastian, 47–48
trade, 129–133, 144

uncertainty, 11, 22, 32, 37–41, 127
universities, 55–59

Printed and bound by CPI Group (UK) Ltd, Croydon, CR0 4YY